Education and the Imagination

Education and the Imagination

RUTH MOCK

With a Foreword by
WILLIAM WALSH
*Professor of Education
in the University of Leeds*

1970

CHATTO & WINDUS

LONDON

Published by
Chatto & Windus Ltd
40 William IV Street
London W.C.2

*

Clarke Irwin & Co. Ltd
Toronto

SBN 7011 1551 3

Printed in Great Britain by
Northumberland Press Ltd
Gateshead

Contents

Acknowledgements   *page* 7

Foreword   9

1 Introduction   13

2 Explanation   18

3 The nature and significance of the
      imaginative faculties   38

4 The factors in education and society
      which inhibit imagination   51

5 The influence of contemporary society
      on educational values and practices   66

6 Imaginative teaching   82

7 The education of imagination   98

8 Conclusion   134

Acknowledgements

The author and publishers make grateful acknowledgement to the following for permission to include copyright material: William Collins & Co. Ltd for Sir Julian Huxley's introduction to Pierre Teilhard de Chardin, *The Phenomenon of Man*; George Allen & Unwin Ltd for Christmas Humphreys, *Zen Buddhism*; Ernest Benn Ltd for A. N. Whitehead, *The Aims of Education*; Harvill Press Ltd for Konstantin Paustovsky, *Slow Approach of Thunder*; Laurence Pollinger Ltd and the Estate of the late Mrs Frieda Lawrence and William Heinemann Ltd for D. H. Lawrence, *The Collected Letters*.

Foreword

Mrs. Ruth Mock's book is much to be welcomed in a period which is marked both by the depreciation of imaginative activity and by a painfully limited conception of the values which should inform and sustain education. Coleridge described the bias towards excellence which education should promote as the effort to 'prejudice the soil towards roses and strawberries'.

In fostering that 'prejudice towards roses' upon which depends the humanity of the individual and the quality of civilisation, the strongest appeal should be to the imagination, the power by which the child prises himself free from the present and loosens the clutch of the immediate. In the imaginative act the child disengages himself from the partial and the broken, 'from the universe as a mass of little parts', and comes to conceive of a larger unity and the more inclusive whole. The now is extended, the here complicated. The pressure of the momentary is relaxed and the actual charged with the possible. Alternative courses of action loom up and define themselves for choice. The source separates from the outcome, and the distance between act and consequence increases. Thus a centre of attribution is established, and the concept of responsibility begins its long and difficult pregnancy. In the *Eleventh Lecture* Coleridge outlines the rôle of the imagination.

In the eduation of children, love is first to be instilled, and out of love obedience is to be educed. Then impulse and power should be given to the intellect, and the ends

9

of a moral being be exhibited. For this object thus much is effected by works of imagination: – that they carry the mind out of self, and show the possible of the good and the great in the human character. . . . In the imagination of man exist the seeds of all moral and scientific improvement; chemistry was first alchemy, and out of astrology sprang astronomy. In the childhood of those sciences the imagination opened a way, and furnished materials, on which the ratiocinative powers in a maturer stage operated with success. The imagination is the distinguishing characteristic of man as a progressive being; and I repeat that it ought to be carefully guided and strengthened as the indispensable means and instrument of continued amelioration and refinement.

Coleridge, it will be seen, gives imagination an importance as an educative agency greater than the attenuated respect given it by most modern educators.

Mrs. Mock's sympathetic and intelligent treatment admirably corrects our current attitude and points the way towards its reform. Imagination, as she shows, is not a garnish of the soul, a mere finish according to a fashionable specific. 'The rules of the imagination are themselves the very powers of growth and production.' The life of the child before school is quick with the propulsive energies of imagination which 'carry the mind out of self'; the duty of the school is to bring before the learner works of imagination of such quality (and science is also a human achievement imaginatively initiated) that 'they show the possible of the good and great in the human character'. The bleakness of so much schooling comes from confining imagination to a cramped parish of aesthetic activity. But imagination is the air in which new knowledge breathes, as it is the salt preserving the savour of the old. 'Knowledge', it has been said, 'does not keep any better than fish.'

FOREWORD

Imagination is so important in education not only ‾ because it is the crown of experience but also because, as George Santayana saw, it is part also of the core of experience. It is the means by which experience is shared. Without it we should stay gaoled in our private darkness. With it we enter into different lives, discover other minds and are made free of their products. To share with another is to be joined to him, and imagination is the great unifier of humanity:

> men's perceptions may be various, their powers of understanding very unequal, but the imagination is, as it were, the self-consciousness of instinct, the contribution which the inner capacity, and demand of mind make to experience.

Imagination breaks down the finitude of personal life and dissipates the illusion of individual selfishness in the interests of a more inclusive reality. A man can say, Santayana wrote, 'I have imagination and nothing that is real is alien to me.' Imagination occupies a middle ground and like art it exists between extremes.

> Between sensation and abstract discourse lies a region of deployed sensibility. . . . This region called imagination has pleasures more airy and luminous than those of sense, more massive and rapturous than those of intelligence.

It is, I suppose, conceivable that imagination could remain simply an inward grace by which the ideal might achieve a perfection impossible in actuality. But 'activity, achievement, a passage from prospect to realisation, is evidently essential to life', and above all to the life of:

11

a creature like man, whose mode of being is a life of experience and not a congealed ideoity; he must operate in an environment in which everything is not already what he is presently to make it.

The transitive force of imagination follows on man's essential incompleteness and on the advantage he has in being born only half-made. Had intelligence been perfected in the womb, nothing important could have been learned afterwards and man would have remained a doctrinaire practitioner of the *a priori*. As it is, it is an instinct in man to bring his humanity to bear upon the world outside himself, and by humanising and rationalising objects to make his habitat expressive of his nature and his intentions. The facts of existence are simply facts, no more than 'the cracklings of an inexhaustible garrulity' until they become symbols, and nothing can make them symbols but an eager imagination on the watch for all that can embody its ideals.

Mrs. Ruth Mock's sensitive and humane book admirably enforces and orchestrates the function and the value of the imagination.

WILLIAM WALSH

Introduction

SINCE it was first published in 1955 I have had a number of requests to amplify my book *Principles of Art Teaching*, which, so that it should not be obscure, I wrote perhaps too simply and concisely. But as soon as I started to think about such an amplification, I realised that I have little more to say about the practical aspect of how to teach art, because having discussed what I believe to be the fundamental principles, their constructive application in general education depends upon the individual teacher's imaginative understanding, both of his subject and of each child, in the context of his own generation.

It is, however, imaginative understanding, and above all, imagination itself, which need further consideration, especially as the visual arts are essential and irreplaceable in education because through them we can educate these faculties. Consequently I decided to explore the meaning of imagination, the efforts which it demands, the disciplines which it imposes, and its significance and function in teaching. It is a word which is used freely in relation to education and in the last decade far more attention has been given to it and to the work of imaginative teachers who are capable of preserving and developing the imaginative faculties of every child. But even these teachers do not always have a full and sure understanding of their purpose and achievement and they may be easily discouraged by irrelevant criticism from uncomprehending parents, fellow teachers and officials. So I believe that we still have insufficient understanding of imagination and of its implications, and even in the context of art teaching, where we should be most alive to its characteristics, it is often neglected or misunderstood.

In recent years I have become increasingly aware of the tremendous importance of imagination, not only in education, but in every sphere of life and activity and it often seems as if every tragedy and evil can be ascribed to a lack of it. To a great extent our lives are dominated by able and quick-witted individuals whose imagination, often through no fault of their own, has since infancy been discouraged or suppressed, and who in consequence, and in spite of their often impressive intellectualism as well as of their declared intent, have little human sympathy or perceptive understanding. Such an intentionally kindly man can be, for example, unintentionally cruel in his support of social or racial injustice when this works to his own interest and when he cannot recognise its true character because his imaginative limitations make him unable to comprehend emotions and conditions of life other than his own.

However limited their intellectual capacity, imaginative and intuitive individuals are capable of sympathetic relationships and understanding which add depth and purpose to their own lives and to the lives of those with whom they come in contact. These include a host of greater and lesser artists and craftsmen (taking both art and craft in their widest meanings) but I am thinking especially of those teachers who may have the slenderest academic qualifications but whose ability and achievement, founded in imagination, is nevertheless considerable. It is tragic that often they have little confidence or realisation of their contribution to education because they are persuaded that academic success is all-important, both for themselves and for their pupils.

Also tragic is the harm which unimaginative, yet efficient, teachers do in a school where their influence is powerful and self-propagating because society has been, and is still being, educated by them to admire and demand wholly rational thought and examinable results.

Whatever may have been achieved by it in the past, we have learned today that the unquestioning obedience demanded by many Victorian parents and teachers can lead to excessive conformity and at worst to totalitarianism, but in trying to establish a democratic society we have not yet succeeded in educating children of all kinds of ability to be both responsive and responsible. We are partially successful with a small number, but we are apt to ignore the importance of enriching the imagination (and consequently the sensibility) of the academically able, while we know little about releasing and developing the imaginative potential in those less gifted in this way. At present the unacademic child is too often deprived of the ways in which he could distinguish himself, and in consequence he is made to feel that he is unable to undertake responsibility or to accomplish anything worthwhile. Yet when his imagination is released and directed he too has the power to assimilate facts and to make sensible decisions, which, although they are realised without rational thought, are nevertheless logical. Imagination is fundamental at all levels of intellectual achievement, and although the intelligence and way of thinking of those incapable of academic reasoning may not be conventional, they are none the less valuable, both to their possessors and to the community.

All education, both in academic subjects and in the arts, is sterile unless it is illuminated by imagination, and in an age of computors and automation, which is already reshaping many a curriculum, we should bring our creative imagination and imaginative understanding to bear upon every scientific and technological achievement, ensuring that each works to our advantage and that we do not become robots manipulated by some remote power. At the same time, the organisation of society is inevitably and increasingly collective, and the assertion of individual consciousness and expression, through the imaginative faculties, is all the more important.

In an article in the *Guardian* in 1966 John Wren-Lewis wrote: 'For it will not be long now – certainly not much after the end of the century – before the computor will begin to move into the realms of higher mental activities. It will be capable of doing our scientific theorising and our invention as well as our engineering and our production planning. From then on it will begin steadily to remove the social premium on brains, just as surely as tools removed the natural premium on brawn at the very beginning of civilisation. The merely brainy will then begin to become redundant, and the only people who really count will indeed be those who, by fortunate chance, if not by really far-sighted training, have been educated in the basic human talents of personal sympathy and social and artistic creativity. These alone will be able to determine that the intellect (human or mechanical) organises useful rather than destructive schemes.'

In writing about imagination I am conscious of my inadequacy. I had an orthodox and unimaginative education which for many years inhibited my development and understanding; I am an art teacher with no scholarly knowledge of such relevant subjects as philosophy and psychology, and even after many years as, I hope, a reasonably imaginative teacher, it has been a struggle to present my ideas coherently. What I have written is the outcome of my own experience; it does not presume to be a philosophical or psychological treatise, and I know that it is limited by my own limitations and that imagination is an attribute which has engaged the attention of formidably erudite and brilliant men. But nowhere have I found imagination related to the practical problems of everyday teaching, and perhaps because I write as a teacher, and often with difficulty, this book may be helpful to others with a comparable education and powers of understanding. Because my subject is the visual arts, I have used them to illustrate my interpretation of the word imagination and my belief that the imaginative faculties can, and should be, rediscovered, fostered and educated, but I hope that teachers of other subjects will be able to translate my opinions into their own terms and that they will find them illuminating.

2

Explanation

Imagination is not the talent of some men, but is the health of every man.

EMERSON.

IN the word imagination there are several shades of meaning which we encounter daily in reading or in conversation, and perhaps because of this we are apt to use the word without precise understanding of it. I am therefore first explaining the aspect of imagination which I believe to be important in education, and also of other words and terms which I shall be using.

From the Oxford English Dictionary it is clear that the meaning of imagination can vary between 'idle fancy: a mental concept which does not correspond to the reality of things or which does not derive from external observation', and the definition: 'The creative faculty of the mind in its highest aspect; the power of framing new and striking intellectual conceptions; poetic genius' with the quotation from Darwin: 'The imagination is one of the highest prerogatives of man. By this faculty he unites, independently of the will, former images and ideas, and thus creates brilliant and novel results.'

The first definition of 'idle fancy', implying a ready means of escape from the discipline of attentive and purposeful observation, has made imagination rightly suspect to many teachers, but the second proves that far from being divorced from reality, imagination heightens it and is an essential factor in education. In

18

this sense imagination is a creative effort – the creation – by an individual of an image or an idea hitherto un-experienced by, or unknown to, him. This image or idea may not be absolutely original, in that no one has ever produced anything remotely like it before, but it is a wholly personal and unique discovery for the individual. It does not come by magic as if from no-where; the person engaged in the act of imagining does not merely conjure up an image, but he makes a con-scious, or more usually an unconscious, selection (this is Darwin's 'independently of the will') from incidents in his past experience and knowledge, relating one to the other so that instead of remaining isolated and fragmentary impressions they are ordered into a new and unified form. He has to suspend his usual prejudices as to the nature and purpose of the facts at his command, he has to dare to advance beyond the limits and security of his present understanding in order to explore new relationships and to arrive at a new synthesis.

Such imaginative effort is not limited to its usual association with works of art. It may in fact have no formal manifestation, but be revealed in independent thought, human relationships and everyday decisions which are in consequence sincere, sensitive and respons-ible. When we say that an adult or child is imaginative we mean that he has these characteristics – that he gives his attention without prejudice to the object of his regard and that his subsequent action or idea originates in his personal understanding and is sympathetic. He is likely to have a considerate relationship with his companions, realising, intuitively if he is young, that they have wishes and impulses comparable with his own; he is interested in objects around him, noticing their particular qualities and being careful not wantonly to harm or destroy them, while he is stimulated by every activity to greater personal effort, using his former experience to further and to integrate his work.

If we believe someone to be unimaginative, we consider that his actions and opinions are founded upon conventions and stereotypes beyond which he dare not go to discover his personal ideas, sympathies or form of expression. He has little sensibility in his approach either to personalities or to objects; he is indifferent to causing damage or destruction; he is over assertive, and whatever his intellectual powers he regards everything with the reserve of preconceived judgment and he becomes increasingly rigid and limited in his understanding.

I am not suggesting that an imaginative individual, whether adult or child, is inevitably a well-behaved and constructive member of any community, and indeed an imaginative child often has temperamental difficulties especially when he is in an alien or unsympathetic environment. But he possesses the faculties which, rightly developed, will enable him to mature into a creative and co-operative personality.

When we say in conversation: 'I can imagine what you mean', we are not implying that we have received miraculous enlightenment. We are in fact saying: 'By drawing upon incidents of my former experience and reassembling them into a new pattern which I have not hitherto considered, I can understand your meaning.'

Conversely, 'I cannot imagine what it is like to be rich' means: 'However deeply I search my memory I am unable to recollect any events and experiences in my past life which could be arranged in some way to give me an understanding of riches.'

In fact to be able to imagine we must have had former experience, but we do not rely upon this alone, for to recreate it in an act of imagination we have to reconsider and relate it to the medium in which we intend to express it.

EXPLANATION

In the arts and sciences creative imagination demands that an individual frees himself from his immediate preoccupations and associates himself with the medium he is using – the paint, wood or stone for the painter or sculptor, the words for the writer, the sounds for the musician or the facts for the scientist – so that with it he creates a new form which may to some extent be unexpected even to himself. He must respect the quality of the medium and handle it so that it develops according to its particular characteristics which he does not destroy by imposing his own, often alien, purpose upon it, forcing it into a preconceived or derivative formula. The medium can suggest, and it sometimes even resolves, the final form of an imaginative work.

A simple example brings creative imagination within the bounds of familiar experience. When an individual of any age embarks, either from direct observation or from memory, upon the painting of a tree, his past knowledge of trees and his appreciation of their characteristics can add to his ability to express in his own way his interest in some aspect of a particular tree. But if he does no more than recollect and reproduce stylised shapes which represent 'tree' in commonplace illustrations, and if to intensify this conventional image he handles his medium according to prescribed rules of how to paint a tree, he does not achieve anything which could possibly be termed imaginative. He merely perpetuates a stereotype and still further dulls his own perception. If, however, he can free himself from the conventional image, see the tree afresh, and realise in it particular qualities which he can express in terms of his medium, he will discover new relationships, both in the forms and colours which embody his conception of the tree and in the physical nature of the medium itself. He will then produce a work which is imaginative, whether or not it is based upon direct observation.

It will be an original work of creative imagination, not because a tree has never before been painted, but because this is peculiarly his vision and interpretation of it in terms of paint. He has looked, seen and consequently he has been able to imagine. This is his original discovery; through his sensibility both to the tree and to the medium he has been able to record some especial characteristic of the tree which he has never before completely realised. We may see comparable paintings of a tree, but we shall never see its exact likeness elsewhere for it is the unique visual experience of a unique individual.

When a painter says that he has worked from imagination, he does not mean that from a set of generally accepted whimsical symbols he has produced a fantasy. Neither has he used his technical accomplishment purposely to shock or to annoy, for he has embarked upon his painting with no preconceived ideas about either his subject or his medium, and with no certainty about the final result, but content to allow this to emerge from relationships which he discovers while he works. He has ignored details irrelevant to his purpose, so that only the significant characteristics of his subject remain, and these are distilled through, and intensified by, his sensibility to them and to his expression of them in terms of his medium. His sensibility is no affectation; it is his ordering and refinement of his sense impressions, and because of the intensity and quality of his selective vision, an imaginative painting is to an observer a revelation of an aspect of the visual world, and it has a far greater impact than one which is factually stated.

In fact although it may not give a precise definition or a realistic representation, creative imagination explores reality, enhances and transcends it, producing an image which is more memorable and significant than any which we recognise factually and convincing us that this is one which is inevitable and true.

For young children and for the few remaining unsophisticated peoples of the world, creative imagination is spontaneous, an immediate and simple response to events and needs. But for others it is a challenging and often uncomfortable activity. There is doubt, uncertainty and perhaps painful mental rejection of familiar and reassuring concepts before the new image or idea is realised. The act of imagination has been described as a leap in the dark and by Arthur Koestler in *The Sleepwalkers* as comparable to the mystic's dark night of the soul, in which the security of former spiritual understanding disappears and there is an agony of loneliness before the dawn of new comprehension.

There are, for example, many innately sensitive individuals who from force of circumstance have always had their thoughts, actions and experiences circumscribed by convention. They may have submitted to a rigorous upbringing and education, or they may have accepted unquestioningly the beliefs and attitudes of their environment – a public-school boy reproduces as exactly the approved idiom of his house and school as the juvenile delinquent the popular expressions of his gang, while the well-to-do business man is as conformist in his neo-Georgian surroundings (or whatever is currently fashionable) as the working-class housewife with her plastic knick-knacks. None has dared to think or to behave in any but the manner orthodox to his group, or to look for anything but the familiar image. Then at some time and for some reason such an individual has the opportunity and urge to think, see and do for himself and in his own way – in fact to act as an imaginative being. The reassessment, and probable rejection, of ideas and values with which he has grown up and which for years have provided him with apparent confidence and security, give him unpleasant doubts and he feels painfully isolated from his former companions to whom his new beliefs and forms of expression are strange and suspect. For many this readjustment is too disturbing and they remain to the end of their lives dominated by convention, frightened by change, and an unquestioning member of their group or gang. But those who dare to discover their personal belief, appreciation and means of expression possess the resources and true confidence which enable them to extend their sympathies and understanding, fearlessly to consider contemporary developments and to become mature personalities.

The ability and will to think and act imaginatively depend to a large extent upon our heredity and education. Those who are born into families with a tradition of independent thought, enquiry and appreciation are more likely to be capable of creative imagination than those whose parents and forebears have been bound by current beliefs and sanctions and who have been visually dead to their surroundings, while children whose school encourages personal initiative, discovery and sensibility have an immense advantage over those whose teacher's aim is to produce conformists to a certain class or sect.

The experience and knowledge which provide the necessary resources for our imagination (both when it is spontaneous and when it is the product of conscious effort) come partly from our education, and partly from events and influences in our environment and society – the human ones of family and school, the natural of climate and countryside, and the man-made of urban life and industrial occupations. Our formal education gives us factual knowledge, it introduces us to the arts and the sciences, and it makes us aware of the discipline and satisfaction inherent in learning. In all this an intermediary is present and necessary in the form of the teacher, the author of the book, the architect, musician, painter or sculptor, and to this extent such experience is second-hand and less vivid. But the events and influences of our environment and society give us a first-hand, wholly personal, experience and form of knowledge. We may or may not be conscious of these but because they have a direct impact upon us they are the more profound and significant in the shaping of our sensibility and understanding and in the provision of resources for our imagination.

We are closely bound to our environment and society, and while we create them and contribute to them, we are at the same time their product, inevitably subjected to their pressures. Thus the tradition and quality of life in a family or a school are created and perpetuated by each member, whose development is at the same time decisively influenced by the established habits and opinions. The personality and achievement of a child today are as surely moulded by the values of his parents, education, and environment, as were those of a Victorian child brought up with an unquestioning accept-ance of authority, and both in their time further the beliefs by which they have been conditioned until they may well become thoughtless conventions. The reaction against such conventions comes from the few individuals of greater imaginative comprehension and understand-ing; thus, while far into this century many children were still brought up in conditions of Victorian authori-tarianism which were meaningless in the context of their own society, the more imaginative parents and teachers had rejected the extravagant aspects of this up-bringing even before the Victorian era was over.

The nature of our response to our environment and society determines the extent and depth of our imaginative ability. When an individual responds to the popularly accepted events and beliefs of his time, his creative imagination derives from, and reflects, aspects of life and understanding which are shared by many of his contemporaries. His experiences are personal, but they are also common to members of his family, town, country, and today even to people of nationalities other than his own; he accepts the current standards of religious belief, morality and education, while his work, although it is his sincere effort and unique expression, reflects popular influences and is in an idiom recognisable to, and acclaimed by, his own society. (I am discounting those of any age who will only accept antiquated forms.) Even if he is engaged in what is for him an objective effort, perhaps joinery or silver-smithing, his approach is qualified by the values of his time and his completed work is inescapably of it, so that by its design and craftsmanship we can establish its date and country of origin. For the same reasons we have the popular movements in the arts which canalise contemporary aspirations and achievements and are a mirror of the era – for example, the Pre-Raphaelites of the later 19th century reflected the literary and moral approach to the arts, the surrealists of the 1920s and '30s the preoccupation with psychoanalysis, and the op. painters of today the interest in scientific technology. When such movements are carried on after they have ceased to reflect popular sensibility and interest, they become the conventions which contribute to sterile traditionalism.

On the other hand, irrespective of his upbringing and environment, an outstanding personality may develop beyond the popular climate of opinion and have a far deeper sensibility to particular influences and to underlying pressures and beliefs. These will be as yet unrealised by his society, and his response to them, and his imaginative work which expresses them will be startling and may well be rejected or reviled by his contemporaries. The man capable of such imagination is profoundly of his time and yet he towers above it; he can be identified as being of a certain nationality and period; he may lead a movement and change the values and practices of his society, but he is supremely individual and he remains a source of inspiration to generations. Amongst educationalists Froebel was such a man, and in the visual arts Leonardo, Rembrandt and Picasso.

All acts of imagination are authentic and meaningful to the creator, but according to the depth of his imagination and to his choice, whether conscious or unconscious, of a popular or a particular influence, his work is the more or less significant to his contemporaries and successors.

For my present purpose I am ignoring the definitions of imagination which imply whimsy or fantasy, for neither has any place in the education of creative imagination.

A whimsy is capricious, related to personal and superficial sentiment with no foundation in disciplined observation or selective thought. It is the unnecessary elaboration of an object or an idea, it stimulates reassuring daydreams and memories, and with an emphasis upon an acceptable half-truth it provides a refuge from the realities of life and from the original art which reflects them.

Unfortunately, and in the name of imagination, whimsies are frequently produced for young children and used in teaching in the belief that they are suitable for the innocence of infancy. But a young child has the true innocence of honest observation and appreciation, he can face reality, and because it is essentially trivial, a whimsy can only limit his development and understanding, conditioning him to prefer futile sentiment.

EDUCATION AND THE IMAGINATION

It is difficult to make a precise definition between fantasy and creative imagination of the kind I am concerned with in education, for certain qualities in each are present in the other. Unlike whimsy, fantasy states categorically, but with sensibility to essential characteristics, that something is what it is not: a mountain is a giant, a cloud a chariot with horses or that a fox is capable of human speech. Imagination examines and intensifies reality while fantasy evades it; fantasy is illusory, communicating an element of unreality and extravagance, which is heightened by the realism with which the juxtaposition of extraordinary concepts is presented, thus making them all the more 'fantastic'.

In a picture of a forest, for instance, in which trees have been transformed into men, the paint is used as realistically as possible to describe the features and expressions of the man and the forms and surfaces of the trees. We are given an explicit statement of the facts and nature of the illusion, which we may enjoy but which even so is less convincing than, for example, Pollaiuolo's 'Apollo and Daphne' or a comparable painting by Marc Chagall in which a woman is partly tree or partly animal. In such paintings the subject is interpreted and expressed both formally and in terms of the medium, and these are works of creative imagination which are haunting and memorable.

It would be a fantasy for me to suppose that I am a wholly different person or in a wholly different situation – a successful politician, for example, or that I am living upon a tropical island. In such a case I would recollect and assemble all the relevant facts so that they appeal to my emotions and present understanding. I should form an irrational concept and enjoy believing myself to be this other personality or in this other situation, but I should do nothing to deepen my understanding of, and sensibility to, either one or the other.

EXPLANATION

But as soon as I do extend by a mental effort my awareness of circumstances other than my own, I am engaged in an act of creative imagination.

In the same way a story for children in which an animal is dressed in human clothes and lives in a house and talks, or in which a car has a human face and sentiments, merely tells us with realistic detail of a fanciful situation. The story may be appealing because of its quaintness, but it adds nothing to our comprehension of either animal, mechanical or human existence.

On the other hand, allegories, myths and legends (and in these I would include fairy stories and such books as *The Wind in the Willows* and those by Beatrix Potter) reflect universally shared experiences and conditions and they deepen our awareness of them. The personalities, animals and natural objects in such stories are used to illuminate the fallibilities, hopes, fears, comedies and tragedies which are common to us all. The fox and the crow in Aesop's fable, for example, underline human greed and vanity, Icarus in the Greek myth our aspirations, and Beauty and the Beast the place of compassion in all our relationships.

These again are memorable; they are works of creative imagination which by increasing our resources of sensibility and understanding develop the same faculties in us. It is this aspect of imagination which I believe to be essential in education.

Imaginative comprehension is a resolved and directed form of intuition, and by it I mean that immediate perception and flash of realisation in which the essential quality and character of the object, idea, personality or situation, which cannot readily be assessed or explained by factual description, is apprehended by an individual and made part of his own experience. This can be a young child's intuitive realisation of the true character of a person – of his severity or kindliness – without the use of reason or an analysis of his reactions to that person's features of mannerisms. Or it can be an adult's immediate recognition of the quality of a man-made or natural object. Without rational thought he responds to the form, colour, tone, texture and to relationships of these, which communicate their significance, whether it be emotional, aesthetic or utilitarian.

Imaginative comprehension is natural to a young child and to those whose imagination has been preserved and educated, and it returns in occasional flashes to many who are otherwise imaginatively inert. As if he has momentarily rediscovered the spontaneous appreciation – in fact the innocence – of his childhood, a usually insensitive adult will suddenly respond to the quality of great music, poetry or painting, and he does this the more readily if the experience is unexpected, giving him no time to take refuge in his habitual prejudices.

This aspect of imagination involves a unity of understanding and response to the whole experience, which is all too often fragmented in current education by our emphasis on analysis. It is the simple and intuitively coherent response, which enables individuals who are incapable of concentrated rational thought to arrive at logical conclusions: a child, for instance, will suddenly, and without any intellectual reasoning, realise the correct solution of a mathematical problem which with conscious thought he would find extremely difficult, or a craftsman with no formal education in calculation has a certainty in his precise, yet instinctive, construction of an object or a building.

Imaginative comprehension is the basis of aesthetic appreciation, making it more sure and immediate. It can be independent of previous experience and intellectual knowledge, taking the form of spontaneous intui-

EXPLANATION

tive understanding, and, as in creative imagination, habitual ways of thinking, looking and listening must be suspended and superceded by an objective attention which demands a personal identification with the idea, object or situation. In this case no new idea or image is created, but because the comprehended factor becomes part of the individual's experience, his resources for creative imagination are increased and enriched.

Imaginative understanding combines rational thought and understanding with imaginative comprehension. It regenerates rational thought, which, instead of remaining drily factual, becomes through its illumination more significant and fruitful. It is present in all appreciation and knowledge: when we read, listen or look without it we do no more than assemble facts, while with it we acquire a purposeful enjoyment and understanding. It should generate criticism and analysis, which in this sequence are constructive, but when, as often happens in education, these are put first and imaginative understanding is secondary or is ignored, our knowledge consists of partially related incidents, it is divorced from our experience and it adds nothing to the maturing of our appreciation.

In fact imaginative understanding forms the essential link between what might otherwise be disconnected sense impressions or meaningless facts. In reading we recognise with our rational mind words, phrases and sentences upon a page, and it is our imaginative understanding which, with resources derived from our previous experience, relates one to another and gives them a memorable and vivid significance. We can, for instance, realise the full poignancy of such a factual statement as: 'there was a dead man carried out, the only son of his mother and she was a widow.' We grow up with words as our means of communication, and with an education centred upon the intelligible and literate use of them, it is for most people easier to exercise imaginative understanding in reading than it is in seeing. But the same faculty is needed in the visual arts if in looking at a painting we are to go beyond a mere identification of the objects to a realisation of the aesthetic qualities and their relationships which determine the expressiveness of the whole work. For example, we could look piecemeal at Giotto's 'Crucifixion', noting first one and then another figure, and arguing that angels with faces distorted by grief are never to be seen in the sky, but we would then experience nothing of the painting's deeper significance or comprehend it as a great work of art.

Imaginative understanding gives an extra dimension to our rational thinking and understanding, making us capable of responding to imaginative truth which is embodied in the arts and cannot be expressed by any other means.

Imaginative truth is far greater than factual accuracy and it gives all learning a coherence which makes us realise the unity underlying knowledge. It can be expressed symbolically, for example, in religious painting and in poetry, or it can be communicated in essence as in music. It is present in all the arts which are not primarily concerned with representation, narrative or propaganda. We may be able to respond to this kind of truth with spontaneous imaginative comprehension, but more often we bring our imaginative understanding to bear upon it.

In the Genesis account of the fall of man, for instance, we are given the full imaginative truth of man's progress from the state of spiritual innocence to that of worldly ambition and knowledge. With only rational understanding we could say that the story is nonsense, and our realisation of the completeness of its sense comes when with imaginative understanding we grasp its basic truth and meaning.

Without imaginative understanding any knowledge or study, however intellectually advanced, can result in limited perception and the consequent danger of opinionated intolerance. This accounts for the arrogance of the members of many sects and for all physical and mental persecution. Christianity becomes nonsensical, even vicious, when it is reduced to factual knowledge and reasoning, and the gruesome academic quibble, for example, of whether or not the Jews betrayed and killed the son of God has resulted in centuries of Jewish persecution and has caused an infinity of human cruelty and suffering, when it has nothing to do with the fundamental imaginative truths about the nature of God and his relationship with man which is conveyed by the New Testament story.

In its proper and constructive character, rational thought necessarily involves all the imaginative faculties, but in the form in which all too often it is accepted in life and education today, rational appreciation, knowledge and understanding mean little more than factual assessment and deduction leading to a precise conclusion. I am limiting myself to this narrow definition which implies that the student or child has a fact, or a series of facts, which he must remember, a process of reasoning which he must master, and a definite result at which he must arrive. He can do this by assembling and memorising the necessary facts and by perfecting the mechanics of deduction, and his achievement can be exactly assessed.

Rational thought of this kind is necessary for the efficient functioning of practical existence in any community. It is the product of immediate physical need for which we plan and provide as soon as and as best we can; we need no more than this limited aspect of rational thought to mend an electric fuse, to memorise a telephone number or to read instructions on an official form.

Such thought is also the basis of any intellectual effort and achievement, but it is only the basis, and if it remains at the level of mental dexterity it never becomes true scholarship. By itself it does not constitute understanding. For this it must be quickened by imagination, and to have any constructive purpose, rational thought and imagination, in all its aspects, must be interactive and interdependent. The greatest men achieve this just balance and relationship.

In writing on *Universities and Their Function* A. N. Whitehead remarks: 'The whole art of the organisation of a university is in the provision of a faculty whose learning is lighted up with imagination.'

Because of our imaginative limitations we are apt to think of the rational and imaginative faculties as being in opposition to one another, the either-ors in individual personalities: either, he is rational and therefore competent, or, he is imaginative and therefore probably ineffectual. But in fact the one complements the other and some degree of each is essential in a mature personality. Concentrated objective attention, which is inherent in imagination, animates the processes of rational thought, while if the vivid sense impressions received through imaginative comprehension are to have any significance beyond that of personal idiosyncrasy, they must be ordered by rational thinking in to a coherent and purposeful pattern. Thus scholarship reaches out beyond the aridly factual, in the arts we are enabled to form aesthetic as well as academic judgments, and knowledge is extended beyond the boundaries and limi-

tations of time into the realm of comprehensive understanding and truth.

I am writing about education in its fundamental sense
as an extension of awareness, as Sir Julian Huxley inter-
prets it in his *Essay of a Humanist*: 'The prime function
of education is not to impart the maximum amount of
factual information, but to provide comprehension, to
help growing human beings to a better understanding of
the world and themselves.'

Every one of us is the focal point of his own experience: we feel ourselves to be the centre of the whole
world which revolves around our apprehension of each
aspect of it. Everything we know, understand or feel
comes from our intellect and senses, in fact from our
response to ideas, objects, personalities and situations
outside ourselves which reflects back to become part
of our individuality and resources.

Each one of us must therefore have the basic awareness of our own physical, mental and emotional potential
and ability. This should not be mere introspection, but a
developing consciousness of ourselves and our faculties in
relation to our environment and society. At certain
stages of our lives, and not only when we are very young
when this is inevitable, we find it difficult to believe that
other individuals have experiences as unique and profound as our own. Other personalities exist only as
adjuncts to ourselves, but to recognise in another an
equivalent centre of awareness is the first step towards
imaginative understanding and consequent maturity.
We have to realise that every one of us is part of, and has
a certain relationship to, our surroundings of which we
are not the dominant centre.

As well as comprehending our place in our environment we must have an awareness of the order and attri-

EDUCATION AND THE IMAGINATION

butes of the natural world, and also of the satisfaction, disciplines and possible achievements in rational thought, imaginative understanding and the creative practice of the sciences and the arts. Finally we must be aware of quality wherever it appears – not only in natural and man-made objects – but also in personalities, relationships and situations.

With an education based upon an extension of awareness we can cater for all abilities, for experience is not narrowed by concentrating on academic knowledge or a limited range of socially or economically rewarding studies. Each individual, whatever his inheritance and attributes, has an ever-increasing and deepening comprehension and understanding. He acquires confidence in himself, his ability, and the contribution he can make to his society, and thus he has the opportunity to develop his full potential.

Awareness is fundamental to all learning. It is comparable to imaginative understanding, for it is made up of imaginative comprehension and some degree of factual knowledge. The first is essential, but the necessary amount of the second depends upon the intellectual equipment of the individual concerned. Great knowledge and powers of rational thought may deepen and increase awareness, and those who have these gifts and combine them with creative imagination are the greatest personalities, scholars, artists and scientists. But those of little intellectual ability and possessing only rudimentary factual knowledge are nonetheless capable of a considerable depth of awareness and of a development of it, although this will never reach into any specialist sphere of scholarship. We must value the qualities and accomplishments of such personalities, discover how to release and extend their imaginative faculties through education, and remember that too great a concern with facts and the skilful manipulation of them destroys spontaneous perception and undermines all aspects of awareness.

Such an approach to education may seem extravagantly romantic or even absurd when, for example, it is considered in relation to the prevailing conditions in an overcrowded urban secondary school. But any such reaction emphasises the extent to which we try to produce pre-determined results and characteristics by imparting facts and imposing standards. By ignoring the presence of awareness in each child we deprive him of the opportunity of developing this from its latent state to one of integrated conscious expression so that it is the basis of his personality and achievement.

Education is concerned with both rational and imaginative thought and understanding and with establishing a constructive balance between the two according to the capacity of each individual. Today, with our computors, teaching machines and language laboratories, we are becoming increasingly efficient at teaching skills and imparting facts, but in the process we are in danger of giving less thought to, and having less understanding of, imaginative powers, their growth and development. Whatever this innate endowment of an individual, I believe that his creative imagination and imaginative comprehension and understanding can be preserved, educated and helped to emerge to play a conscious part in his personality and activity. These faculties are with us in our earliest years, and they remain the attributes of young children, rightly educated older ones and some adults, to all of whom an intuitive relationship with natural objects, other personalities and their environment is as natural as breathing or sleeping.

3

The Nature and Significance of the
Imaginative Faculties

. . 'Tis Contemplation teacheth knowledge truly how to know,
And Reinstates him on his throne, once lost . . .
WILLIAM BLAKE: *Then She Bore Pale Desire.*

IN my own childhood the development of my imagination and of my understanding of its possible scope
and implications was dulled by values which I am often
surprised to find persisting in education today. I was
brought up to admire, even to revere, the arts of the
past, and on a descriptive and moral level I was conditioned to respond to them. But I did not know how
to read, listen or look without prejudice and with
imaginative understanding and I was ignorant of the
creative art of my own time, for my teachers were suspi-
cious of these and did not acknowledge the validity of
imaginative experience which in their opinion was
neither genuine nor a true discipline. They must in fact
have shared the belief of a public school master who
wrote on a boy's report: 'He has too much imagination
which must be suppressed at all costs.'

Later I was influenced by those extreme romantics,
in human relationships as well as in the arts, who associ-
ate imagination with unresolved emotion and self-
centred sentiment. Among these were the ardent disciples of free-discipline and free-expression who would
have been amazed to be termed sentimental, but their
excessive, and often unsubstantiated, claims were based
upon subjective sentiment rather than upon objective

reality. For this reason they alienated rather than convinced me; they emphasised indiscriminate experience at the expense of selective sensibility, and in the chaos of classroom, community or home it was often difficult to discern any purpose or sense of direction save that of the survival of the fittest and the most assertive. I saw how, when each is encouraged to express freely and without restraint his desires and emotions, it can only be the strongest personalities who will enjoy that freedom, for the weaker, trodden physically and spiritually underfoot, can have no share in it.

At the other extreme were those friends and teachers whose conception of imagination was in terms of 'idle fancy', which although a legitimate definition is useless in education. This is the whimsical interpretation centred around conventional prettiness, for example jingles, ditties and illustrations of such subjects as bluebell woods and sunsets. The contemplation of a bluebell wood or a sunset can indeed be, and often is, a profound experience and the beginning of imaginative development, as can the contemplation of anything in nature from a caterpillar to a cow. But, while it is likely that the protagonist of free discipline will be determined to prefer the cow to the sunset, the purely sentimental admirer of the sunset finds nothing of beauty or wonder in the caterpillar or the cow. He is incapable of detaching himself from his subjective feelings and of looking with respect and visual interest. He sees the caterpillar as disgusting, the cow frightening, and both as commonplace. He can respond to the literal idea of an awe-inspiring spectacle and all its emotive associations, and the sunset (or the reassuring representation of it) gives him comfortable thoughts about goodness, beauty and love which do not impinge inconveniently upon his habitual thought and behaviour and which therefore do not have to be resolved. They bolster up his self-esteem, they make him satisfied with his taste, and consequently they inhibit rather than develop his imaginative faculties.

Gradually, through my own work and teaching, I realised that true efforts of the imagination have nothing to do with subjective sentiment in whatever guise it may appear. In adults these efforts demand considerable discipline, first of our rationally educated, materially conditioned brains to achieve the necessary detachment and suspension of personal prejudice and judgment so that we may take a step forward into a hitherto unexplored realm of experience with no certain knowledge of where we shall be led. Then we must have respect and patience in an effort of concentrated attention which may not yield results measurable by any material standard or for a considerable length of time.

These are outward-going exercises in effort and appreciation, and in identifying ourselves with the object of our regard as well as, in the case of the creative arts, with our medium. Ultimately, and inevitably, the outward-going effort reflects back to enrich our inward sensibility, transforming us from a state of lesser awareness to a greater, and modifying or even destroying our former prejudices.

The scope and implications of the imaginative faculties are unrestricted by time or material considerations. However practically advantageous it may be in social or economic progress, wholly rational thought is limited by the boundaries of our intellectual ability in our own society and age. A politician or a banker is, for example, inescapably the product of his nationality and era which condition his thinking and determine his achievement. His work is important and materially beneficial to his contemporaries and often to his descendants, but fifty years after his death it is a factual record and an episode in history.

On the other hand a work of art, or any work produced

by the constructive relationship between imagination and rational thought, appeals to our senses as well as to our intellect and knows no barriers of time and space. Because it too is produced by a certain individual of a certain generation and nationality, it must also reflect and be the outcome of the influences of these, but it is limitless in its significance and power of communication. Not only do we enjoy it, whatever the date and place of its origin, but through it we develop a deeper perception and understanding of our own time and environment as well as that of another age and civilisation, for any work of imagination remains forever as expressive as on the day on which it was created.

A child visiting the Egyptian and Greek galleries in the British Museum will learn far more than dates and the names of kings, temples and tombs. He will sense the differences between the two civilisations, for although he may enjoy looking at the ram of Amen as much as at the head of the horse of Selene, each will tell him of the sculptor's particular perception which was conditioned by the beliefs and values of his time and which produced a wholly different conception of an animal – the one serenely aloof and the other alive with nervous energy. He will have the same experience in looking at the statues of gods, goddesses, kings and queens. Both the head of the Greek goddess Demeter and that of the Benin Queen Mother are convincing and impressive, but each tells of a way of life peculiar to the sculptor's civilisation.

As adults most of us have to make a conscious effort if we are deeply to appreciate the arts or any aspect of the natural world, making them part of our evolving experience. To comprehend an unfamiliar poem, for example, we must first read it as a whole, willing to receive its impact and suppressing incidental criticism based upon our prejudices about the nature of poetry, what is beautiful in literature and all such intrusive detail. We have to trust the writer, to believe that he is sincere and that he possesses different, and greater, discernment and sensibility than our own. We are sharing his experience and what he has created from it, and we should approach this with gratitude and respect. We have to learn to respond to the essential whole and not to be distracted by petty particulars to which we attach disproportionate importance. If we are capable of all these efforts, then we develop in imaginative understanding. As Andre Gide writes in *Pretexts*: 'I have read a certain book . . . there were certain words which I cannot forget. They have penetrated me so deeply that I cannot separate them from myself . . . I am no longer the one I was before I met them . . .'

We have to approach the visual arts in the same way, looking first at the whole work, accepting the impact of the artist's visual sensibility, welcoming the experience of seeing anew through his eyes and forgetting our own humdrum way of looking and ideas as to how objects should be represented. We must, in fact, wholeheartedly give our attention, for if we look at a painting, for example, with our usual prejudices, we expect to see in it something with which we are already familiar. We concentrate on what we like and understand, however limited that may be, and ignore or abuse anything which we do not immediately recognise. Consequently any original work of art is bound to disappoint, if not to annoy, us because it presents a unique sensibility and powers of expression which cannot be anything like our own. For the painter's experience and achievement to increase our visual enjoyment many of us have consciously to clear from our manner of looking all prejudice and prejudgment.

Young children, some older ones and some adults are capable of such an unprejudiced and imaginative response to a work of art. Some years ago I left a reproduction of Rouault's 'Old King' to be framed in a shop which was by a bus stop in a small town. When I collected it the framer said he was very sorry to part with it; it had been in his window, and many of the country people waiting outside for their 'buses had admired it and, never having seen anything like it before, had come in to talk to him about it. They, and the children I was teaching at that time, felt the sombre power of Rouault's conception of the king, they enjoyed the glowing colour, the use of black and the rich surface of the paint, and they entertained none of the niggling doubts of a self-conscious critic: 'The arm is out of proportion. What is he supposed to be wearing? I've never seen a king look like that before.'

A child today will approach with direct imaginative appreciation an example of op art, giving his attention wholly to the visual experience without demanding descriptive subject matter.

Words have both rational and imaginative significance, and so have forms, tones and colours, and to respond to both aspects of them is not only legitimate but necessary. An understanding of the rational without an awareness of the imaginative can only give an expert the ability to identify an object or a painting by his carefully acquired information about its name, date and style, and subsequently to assess its value, while the in-expert will, with no humility or respect, repeat the parrot cry of: 'I don't know any thing about art, but I know what I like' or 'Why can't he paint what I see?' – implying that his commonplace vision is sufficient and must prevail. Or, now that it is a good commercial proposition to acquire works of art, exhibitions are full of spectators who rarely look or are receptive to the impact of the painter's unique visual experience. They earnestly study their catalogues to learn the facts, prices, and the theories of the critics (all of which they can assimilate with limited rational understanding) and they raise their eyes only to read the number on the next picture.

It is possible to enjoy a work of art solely through our imaginative comprehension of it, knowing nothing of the facts of the artist's life and of his technique. But such knowledge, in a proper relationship with our imaginative faculties, can, and should, heighten our appreciation, and without it there is a danger that our response will be but a medley of diffuse impressions which need some degree of rational knowledge if they are purposefully to be integrated into the sum of our experience. We cannot evaluate an individual's aesthetic discrimination, but we can reasonably believe that the sensitive observer of, for instance, El Greco's 'Agony in the Garden' who knows something of the painter's life and development, his use of his paint as well as of his religious belief and his interpretation of the Christian story, has a more permanent and meaningful appreciation than one who knows nothing. The observer's imaginative understanding generates constructive analysis and criticism which deepen the quality of his perception.

An objective response to a manifestation of nature is perhaps the most demanding, although few of us realise or would admit this. In any work of art the creator is present, in the fact of his work if not in person, to substantiate his individual experience, and this is a challenge, and sometimes also an irritant, to the observer. We have to look, listen or understand through someone else's sensory awareness, and to comprehend an original idiom or form of expression is an effort and a discipline. But nature is defenceless before a sentimental approach and we can project our subjective emotions into natural objects, sea or landscapes, and endow animals with whimsical attributes, for none can counter the fancies we impose upon them. We dress monkeys in bonnets, poodles in coats, and our affection for these unfortunate animals seems to be in proportion to their ability to lose their true characteristics. Yet if we are to develop an increasing appreciation of the inherent characteristics of all that we see and experience in nature, we have to make a positive effort of objective attention which is all the more difficult because we are without the statement of a creative artist to direct and discipline our sentiment.

We may not realise the full significance of a work of art, or the quality of some aspect of nature, for a long time, as long as years perhaps, but by containing it in our memory, often without much conscious thought, its significance grows with our growth and assists our growth, until at last from living patiently with incomprehension we reach full comprehension. Many a child will, for instance, respond to form in sculpture, colour in painting, rhythm and sound in music and words in literature when he has little or no understanding of them and certainly could not explain his preferences. Before he identifies a Henry Moore reclining figure as a woman, he enjoys the forms and surfaces which, like exploring a cave, lead him to an awareness of the whole work; without troubling to name the objects he is absorbed by the colour in a Bonnard still-life painting, and when he is still too young to formulate the words he delights in singing. In poetry the alliteration in Gerard Manley Hopkins' 'Wind-hover' and the refrain in T. S. Eliot's 'Hollow Men' appeal to a child's imaginative comprehension although they are rationally unintelligible to him. But even though half-forgotten they will enrich and remain with him until later in his life they emerge into his conscious understanding to give him sudden assurance in his grasp of imaginative truth.

In her last broadcast Baroness Asquith quoted the words which at the age of six awoke in her a love of poetry: 'multitudinous seas incarnadine', and she added: 'I had no idea what it meant and I didn't want to know.'

The lapse of time between approximate comprehension and full imaginative understanding means that true attentiveness is required, not a tense straining after results – the Prussian drill kind of attention – but the identification of our sensibility with the person, object or situation to which we are giving our attention. This is not an instant, thoughtless obedience, a conditioned reflex, or even an erudite deduction, but the quiet consideration and regard which is an outward-going effort of appreciation and understanding, and which requires humility in our willingness to consider an original point of view or idiom. In this there is no preoccupation with prejudice, speed or calculable reward. As well as being true attention this is also true observation.

The giving of attention is as important in lucid rational thought as it is in the imaginative processes. We must be able to reject the ease and comfort of both the purely factual and the sentimental response, and to venture away from our habitual thoughts and opinions to an objective appreciation and consequently an imaginative experience.

The passage of time helps us to distinguish between legitimate and illegitimate forms of art and experience, for time generally reveals the shoddy and the bogus. In the clamour of current claims and controversy many things demand our notice and become imprinted upon our consciousness, and it is difficult, if not impossible, to know what has permanent value. But anything, from the fine arts to the popular, which is merely a product of fashion looks quaint, absurd or is forgotten after ten years during which time the genuine has preserved its quality.

It is important that patient attention – this living with incomprehension which in time leads to comprehension – should be accepted as a matter of fact and never enveloped in an aura of romanticism which fosters a whimsical pride in unproductive chaos. This is the attitude of those who imply: 'I can never understand, I'm always in a muddle, but I'm so sensitive, imaginative . . . an artist.' True attention which results in an extended sensibility and imagination demands direction of our mental and sensory powers, and in the creative arts such attention to both the subject and the medium is the necessary constraint without which the imaginative faculties deteriorate into whimsy. This I shall be discussing more fully in chapter 6.

To T. S. Eliot's 'True poetry can communicate before it is understood' could be added 'True art can communicate and never rationally be understood.' The question 'What does it mean?' in relation to any of the arts is in itself meaningless, for rational, factual meaning, even in the form of narrative or representational description which ultimately may increase our understanding and appreciation, has no part in our primary response to a work of art. One of my formative experiences was when, at the age of about 17, I confided in an intellectual relative my enthusiastic discovery of T. S. Eliot's poetry. I can vividly remember his finger prodding the page of 'Ash Wednesday' and his scornfully repeated query: 'What does it mean? Tell me, what exactly does it mean?' I could not possibly explain the exact meaning of such a line as 'The infirm glory of the positive hour' but in it and the whole poem was a verbal splendour, suggestive of imaginative truth, which was a revelation to me, and I was instantly and finally convinced of the futility of such a question.

Factual knowledge may, as I have said, give us a wider appreciation, but, especially in looking at paintings, many of us have purposely to ignore the narrative or descriptive content if we are to enjoy the visual properties. In our youth we were encouraged to look for the story in a picture (and unfortunately many books for children on art appreciation are still presented in this way) so that it is difficult for us to see anything in, for example, Raphael's 'Crucifixion' but a detailed description of the New Testament story. Yet this is primarily a great visual work of art and if we can respond to its colour, composition and sense of space we will ourselves develop in visual sensibility and imagination. We need not understand or accept Christian dogma, and the painting will always be valued as a masterpiece even if Christianity were wholly to disappear and be forgotten.

By an ordered selection from his past experience, by relating this to the object or idea of his present interest to which he gives an expressive form by his handling of his medium, the artist is communicating to our imaginative being through our senses of sight, touch or hearing. We grow in imagination if we make the effort of an objectively attentive response, and we shrink if we cling to opinionated prejudices based on the limitations of our rational or sentimental understanding.

In an observer capable of disciplined attention, his imaginative growth is not limited to his relationship with the one subject of his immediate concern. Imperceptibly the necessary humility, respect and patience extend from the particular to embrace other aspects of art and natural creation, restoring the imaginative relationship between man and man, man and nature and man and created objects, and bringing a mature sensibility to the evils of wanton destruction and injury, whether they be mental or physical. When we have only a factual knowledge of evil, and when it in no way affects our own lives, it is possible to tolerate or ignore it, but when we comprehend or understand it imaginatively, it is intolerable.

All this may appear remote from ordinary children and adults and from what they are generally supposed to be and to understand. But it has to do with imaginative and sympathetic relationships and understanding, such as exist naturally in young children and unsophisticated people and which the quick-witted, whose very mastery of rational thought is often a barrier to imaginative understanding, would do well to rediscover. We do not need to look back nostalgically to the small community in which each individual had the dignity of playing an essential and acknowledged part. For most of us the integrated and comprehensible environment which fosters mutual regard has gone and it is fruitless to mourn it, but the imaginative faculties persist, deeply buried though they may be beneath a morass of mental and aesthetic sludge. In earlier centuries and in other civilisations these faculties were recognised and cultivated, yet because they were unrelated to rational thought, they were often allied to superstition and cruelty, while the material conditions of life were brutish. Now we emphasise the rational and material at the expense of the imaginative, but, if we could establish a just relationship between them, we would have a more constructive basis for living than the prevailing rational-materialistic one, and we would give lasting purpose to those humanitarian impulses expressed in many aspects of medical and scientific achievement which are in constant danger of annihilation by parallel destructive ones in the same fields. We would then indeed be nearer true civilisation.

By imaginative teaching I believe that the imaginative faculties can be rediscovered and redeveloped, and in certain classes and in some schools I have seen the leaven of imagination working to produce a more lively, creative, sympathetic and intelligent community. But although the number of such classes and schools is increasing they are still in the minority and their achievement is all the more admirable because every teacher and every child is under constant pressure from contemporary values and opinions, many of which make the exercise and education of imagination difficult and sometimes even impossible. We must therefore recognise and understand the nature of these pressures and the extent to which they influence us and undermine creative methods of teaching.

4

The Factors in Education and Society which Inhibit Imagination

Let me only be still, and know that we can force nothing, and compel nothing, can only nourish in the darkness the unuttered buds of the new life that shall be.

D. H. LAWRENCE: *The Collected Letters.*

ALL efforts of the imagination depend not only upon inherited gifts, but upon personal knowledge and experience which we acquire through our education and by identifying ourselves, either actively or in contemplation, with situations, personalities, objects and events in our environment. For this we must have opportunity, time, and a degree of quiet and solitude, and these conditions are also necessary if our knowledge and experience are to mature, to work upon our awareness and become consciously realised. At the same time we must have confidence to accept the impact of our experience, to trust in its significance, and in some way to express creatively, and however unconventionally, our consequent imaginative comprehension or understanding.

The teachers who try to provide these opportunities and to instil this confidence into their pupils are handicapped not only by the beliefs of our commercially-inspired society but also by the educational traditions which are encouraged and approved by that society.

Our system of education has inherited a strong academic bias which encourages us to attach more importance to results than to the efforts by which we obtain those results, in fact to factual knowledge rather than to sensory experience and awareness, so that through these we have little chance to develop our powers of imagination, and little confidence, or indeed interest, in what powers we do possess.

Many of us have received a form of academic education which, at its best, and if we are educable in this way, promotes a love of learning for its own sake, stimulates intellectual and creative thought and develops to the full our rational resources. But even at its best, its successful products are likely to be limited in their imaginative ability. They do extremely well in their school and university careers, they prosper in all the professions which demand the mastery and communication of facts, and yet they are often unable to appreciate contemporary developments and achievements. At a fairly early age they retreat into the security of the past, relying upon the established facts and conventions of their youth. The best advertisements of such an education were often failures at school, for example Michael Faraday and Albert Einstein, in whom reason was constructively combined with imagination, making them slower but more profound in their development and less able to conform to conventional scholastic standards.

But these are the outstanding personalities; for most of us a classical education is vitiated by our own limitations as well as by those of our teachers, and it is only perpetuated because of our lack of imaginative understanding and because within our national tradition any form of it, however paltry, is socially desirable. In its weakest manifestation, to which I was subjected, the aim is to acquire what A. N. Whitehead in *The Aims of Education* calls ' "inert ideas" – that is to say, ideas that are merely received into the mind without being utilised, or tested, or thrown into fresh combinations.'

Every child has to learn facile methods of thought and reasoning and how to assemble and reproduce inert ideas so that he may pass examinations and unprotestingly fit into contemporary society. To this end many of us have stumbled through the great works of literature with copious critical and analytical notes, and we have plodded through the ages of art history learning facts and dates and perhaps studying the composition of pictures and the structure of buildings. We have become adept at critical analysis, but because this has preceded, instead of followed, our imaginative understanding, most of the facts are quickly forgotten and we have little appreciation of creative personalities far greater than ourselves whose experience and achievement could well illuminate the problems of our own development and those of our time. Indeed the facts and criticism only serve to build a barrier between us and the impact of any whole work, personality or situation, while our facility in a limited aspect of rational thought makes it increasingly difficult for us to trust in the authenticity of our sensory perceptions.

To return to the child visiting the British Museum; if he has been over-stuffed with historical facts and perhaps aesthetic criticism he will be looking anxiously for evidence of this, and he will find it difficult to have an imaginative comprehension of the qualities of life and belief conveyed by the sculpture of the different civilisations. And when I was an art student my study of architecture was limited to memorising the measurements of the Doric, Ionic and Corinthian orders and to reproducing these in an examination. For years this arithmetical exercise prevented me from developing any appreciation of spatial qualities in architecture.

We are persuaded during our formative years that factual evidence and reasoning are all-important and this belief is strengthened by every contact with contemporary society in which material success and power predominate.

We live in an age of commercial-materialism, and it is both foolish and hypocritical to decry the great material advantages which commerce has given us or to deny that they represent a higher standard of living, for we should all be loath to forgo them. But we should realise how commercial interests permeate and shape our lives and the extent to which they determine our values and hold us in fee. We might think that material independence would give us a comparable independence of thought and initiative, but in fact we come to rely upon the ease and comfort which in everyday life diminish physical and mental challenge. We are lulled by them into a ready acceptance of ideas and values which are propagated by commerce and which are necessary to its survival, but which are irrelevant, if not destructive, to our imaginative being. Such ideas are conventional and the values are approximate, and in fact they cannot afford to be original or particular, inspiring individual belief, behaviour or objective attention, for they must persuade us to accept and conform to commercial standards, to have a self-centred and sentimental response, to believe that the so-called facts are true and important, and that to be happy we must have more and more material possessions however shoddy these may be.

Imagination is suspect and often actively discouraged by those who manipulate a commercial society, for imaginative personalities are the misfits, apparently perverse in their interests and judgments which upset statistical calculations. So each of us is under continual pressure to reject the unique sensory and imaginative experience which would make us different from our companions, and which would convince us that, for instance, a high standard of living cannot be measured in material terms alone – how often we go to the hairdresser, or whether we have one car or two – but that it also depends upon how much opportunity we have for creative work, reading, listening to music, exploring our environment, making new friends and understanding new situations. Gradually, and however soon they may be denied or superceded, we come to accept the spate of half-truths which provide a soothing escape from the efforts of personal enquiry and initiative, and we find spurious security in surrounding ourselves with gadgets and fashionable objects for which, however, we have no deep affection and do not even look at intently. In fact our dustbin economy depends upon everything being thrown away as soon as it shows any sign of wear, while the propaganda for contemporary modes of thought and appreciation is so intense that homes, formerly full of possessions which were so much the choice and delight of their owners that they reflected their personalities, are now as anonymous as any furniture shop.

Even more significantly contemporary customs and scientific technology are committing a large number of us to a life of partial awareness in which we shun or are denied the most profound and formative experiences. In western countries the efficiency of social services and of medical care not only mercifully protect most of us from the extremes of pain and poverty, but they, and our own increasing fastidiousness, also withhold from us personal contact with dissimilar or unpleasant conditions of life, eccentricity, and even from the greatest of all experiences, birth and death, which destroy every barrier, heighten our perception and make us almost intolerably vulnerable to every sensory impression. At one time every one lived in full consciousness of the rich, albeit anguished, pattern of life, but now we are able to turn politely away from any event which might prove disturbing.

On an everyday level modern transport and amenities insulate us against elemental forces, while prefabrication, labour-saving equipment and mass-produced and packaged foods isolate us from natural materials and a consequent appreciation of their particular quality. Unless we are provided with such experiences at school (and these are never as meaningful as those which come to us naturally through our environment) every city-dweller could go through life unaware of the efforts and knowledge which were commonplace to his forebears. He is only partially conscious of the changing seasons; the efficiency of street lighting is an absolute barrier between him and the vastness of the night sky, and few know what it is like to walk long distances in the wind, rain or snow, to dig deep into the earth, or even, on an apparently trivial scale, to make a good darn. I mention these with no puritanical belief in the benefit of primitive and often uncomfortable experience, but because such efforts exercise us mentally and physically. Through them we acquire a personal knowledge of (and often a delight in) the physical world, of the quality of the element or substance with which we come in contact, and we have the satisfaction of physical achievement. In these are the roots of imaginative experience and development. Several decades ago we welcomed the disappearance of tiring and time-consuming tasks, believing that this would provide for a fuller and more creative life, but such has not been the result for neither imaginative understanding nor creativity can flourish without resources and in a vacuum, especially as suggestions for filling this are readily offered by commercial interests, so that the time which is saved is often spent in purposeless occupations.

Television, which has drawn children indoors and away from pavement and garden play, is the most general and popular time-filler today. Through it we

can to some extent participate in world events, it makes
a factual contribution to our understanding, and it gives
us an interest in international affairs and a greater
tolerance of different ways of life for which it may be
capable of arousing our sympathy – although I sometimes wonder whether the sight, for instance, of starva-
tion or suffering safely confined within the familiar
dimensions of the screen and presented in the same way
as fiction does little more than accustom us to the idea
of it. I believe this to be especially true of a child, who
in consecutive programmes may see a man killed in a
thriller and a one killed in an actual war. He does not
clearly differentiate between the two incidents, and the
real man undergoing an agonising death arouses in him
no greater feelings of compassion and distress than the
murder of the fictional one.

Television is the one influence, common to us all
today, which replaces the social, religious and political
meetings and festivals which were potent experiences in
the past. A televised programme must have a popular
appeal, it must be generally acceptable and comprehensible and it cannot have those particular and peculiar
characteristics which, for better or worse, formerly
generated unique qualities in towns, villages and
families and gave every district its regional flavour. Now
we are apparently better informed, more rational and
tolerant, and these are undoubtedly valuable attributes,
but for the nourishment of our imaginative being we
are acquiring only second-hand experience and an
approximate vision which we grow to accept as reality.
We will say: 'I've seen the State Opening of Parlia-
ment . . . the Olympic Games . . . bird life in the
Hebrides . . .' with the implication 'I know all about
that', when we have in fact missed the original visual
experience in its depth and complexity and with the
addition of particular sounds, smells and the sense of

confinement or space which our selective sensibility finds significant. It is easier to watch an event on television than to go to it, so indolently we sit at home where no physical, mental or sensory effort is required of us.

I have been told of a boy who was terrified by a story which he heard on the radio, but when he saw the same story on television he was unmoved. This I believe was intended to demonstrate the superiority of television over sound radio for children, but although I would never wish a child to be frightened, it proved to me that in the first instance the boy had to use his imagination to follow the story which in consequence became over-whelmingly vivid, whereas on television every detail was provided for him and the story became another un-remarkable tale.

We accept television as a visual medium, but, what-ever else we may get out of it, there is little which is visually memorable or stimulating. It supplies us with a profusion of factual images which we can label as, for example, 'submarine', 'elephant' or 'policeman', but only rarely are we presented with a truly visual experi-ence which provokes our sense of wonder and imagina-tion. Fortunate exceptions are several programmes for children, especially those in which original, and imagina-tive, drawings are used, but on the whole all that we see or hear is pre-selected for us with the intention that it should be unexceptional, while background music is intended to condition our emotional response. We have nothing but second-hand experience, nothing is acutely or personally realised, everything becomes tolerably familiar, and we are increasingly apathetic in making the efforts of imagination which lead to fuller under-standing.

Even if we have the opportunity for personal experi-ence, its supplements of time, quiet and solitude are difficult to find. Today all time is full of the drumming insistence of time itself – time to start, time to stop, time to do the next thing – and by our acceptance of its importance we increase the relentless pressure of speed: how quickly can we travel from a to b, how many jobs can we get through in a certain length of time, how soon can we finish work, or how many cities can the businessman visit in one week. Instead of giving us more time to spend according to our personal choice, gadgets and modern transport have created a tyranny of time, with the emphasis on how much is done rather than on the manner in which it is done, and it is impossible to give our whole attention to the effort, object or situation with which we are concerned. We are eccentrics if we choose to travel slowly (whether physically or mentally) allowing our sensory impressions to penetrate and permeate our consciousness. To stand and stare is lunatic inefficiency, and there is no chance to ponder over qualities we see, smell, hear or touch. We need tranquillity for the growth of our imagination and for this we should have boundless and permissive time, but today it engulfs and enmeshes us.

In some occupations we have to spend considerable lengths of time passively, concentrating on efficient repetitive action which prevents all but the most trivial thoughts. Those of us who are fortunate in not having to work at a mechanical job in a factory, may nevertheless have a similar experience in driving a car, when safety demands that we give all our attention to the competent handling of it, and when any imaginative thought or appreciation of our surroundings might well be fatal to ourselves or to others. For a few, mechanical occupations are stimulating and provide time for creative thought (for instance, the writers who become taxi-drivers so that they have time to think) but for most of us they are merely exhausting and leave us with no energy or inclination for objective attention, so that time passes without anything being added to our imaginative resources.

Today noise is a positive presence assuming an almost material form. Natural noise – the sound of children or of animals, the cries of a crowd or the crashing of a storm – has variety in its tone and strength, it is expressive of an emotional or elemental content and it is the contrast which emphasises quiet and our realisation of it. However much we may dislike natural noise, it is a facet of human experience, contributing to our awareness and understanding. But nowadays the prevailing noise is mechanical, unremitting and overwhelming; the noise of jet aircraft and mechanical drills, of traffic, transistors and machinery, in which it is impossible to look, listen or think with perception or to any purpose. We can appreciate to what extent we have come to accept noise when we remember that in the early years of this century straw was laid in the road to deaden the sound of wheels and of horses' hooves when there was illness or death in the neighbourhood. Now we are born, live and die in constant clamour.

In *Slow Approach of Thunder*, the second volume of his autobiography, Konstantin Paustovsky writes: 'I worked near a circular saw. The sound sent cold shivers down my spine and filled me with ungovernable rage. It drilled through my brain . . . Its mere existence was an insult to man, to human brains, hearts and nerves; when occasionally it stopped, the strain of waiting for it to start again was almost worse.'

Those who live and work in loud and persistent noise must, for self-preservation, come to terms with it, and in fact most of us are so accustomed to noise that we no longer hear, for example, traffic or background music. But in this we are the poorer. We have become partially insensitive to sound, we are no longer aware of the quality of quiet – or we are frightened of it – and although not positively deaf we have lost our keen sense of hearing.

Contemplation, by which I mean the giving of our attention in any sensory effort or in lucid rational thought, is impossible in a tremendous din, and today we are also beset by a visual clamour and restlessness which is as distracting and destructive as an aural one. There is little visual serenity in our man-made environment, and if we are not surrounded by ever-moving crowds and traffic, some image or message is persistently forced upon our attention by advertising, newspapers, magazines or television. We may become so used to these conditions that, although no longer truly seeing them, we are at a loss without them, or we may reject them, but in either case our vision is deadened, for both our passive acceptance as well as our rejection creates a barrier between us and all that we could observe and add to our visual memory.

In our sensory powers we are in fact parodies of what we should be, for along with our hearing and seeing have gone, though for other reasons (among them synthetic materials and frozen and sterilised foods), our acute senses of touch, taste and smell, so that imaginatively we have crippling limitations which pervert and stunt our growth and make the development of mature powers of imagination a remote ideal.

We should be alive and receptive to every sensory impression, which must subsequently be recollected in solitude if it is to be made part of our imaginative experience. Yet nowadays solitude is not considered a desirable state, for it is wrongly confused with a negative condition of loneliness resulting either from a deliberate withdrawal, or an unfortunate isolation, from human company. But as quiet is both the necessary counterpart to noise and has its own positive and constructive characteristics, so solitude is not only the contrast which reveals the pleasures of companionship. It also gives us the opportunity to realise our resources, consciously to construct something from our past experience, and in some degree to face our own personality and to discover our identity.

Today many live in mental, as well as physical, loneliness, unable to find human sympathy in overcrowded living conditions or in the jostle of public transport and city streets. In new housing developments it is difficult to establish neighbourliness and a sense of community in high blocks of flats where contacts have to be made vertically rather than horizontally, where children cannot play together outside their own homes and yet in sight of parents, and where the personal interest, and often solace, of occupations such as gardening, pigeon fancying or rabbit-breeding are impossible or forbidden.

Such loneliness is destructive, not only to personal happiness and confidence but also to purposeful solitude, to which we can withdraw only from the security of well-adjusted human relationships and community life, or from an inner personal maturity which is usually the outcome of these states. An unhappy individual is incapable of being constructively alone, and in most crowds of human beings today there is merely degradation, with none of the robust neighbourliness and companionship which should be generated by human contact. No one, for example, could be said to possess his birthright of human dignity in a London underground train in the rush hour, or upon an escalator which could well be a nightmare conveyor belt to imaginative, if not to physical, annihilation.

Alone we are apt to be deadeningly alone while in a crowd we are isolated one from another, mere numbers being too great for each of us to feel a responsible and respected part of the community. We are rarely in true solitude but only in that state of loneliness which makes no contribution to our resources and increases our fear of relying upon those few we do possess. Creative communal life is founded upon the resources of each individual from which he makes his contribution to the group, as well as upon his powers of sympathetic co-operation and understanding. All these stem from his imaginative faculties which are nurtured in solitude, and thus we are caught in a vicious circle: we have lost the solitude in which our imaginative self can mature, and therefore we cannot create the constructive community life from which we can confidently withdraw to fruitful solitude.

We have become so accustomed to speed, noise and crowds that we are bewildered, even frightened, if we have to go slowly, be quiet or be alone. The quick, superficial action is preferable, and apparently more efficient, than the slower, deeply considered one. Silence is intolerable, so we must have background music, and as our ears have lost their sensibility to small natural noises we must take a transistor radio into the country or to the sea. If we are alone we anxiously fill the void with television or by attaching ourselves to any kind of a group, giving and receiving little but clinging to it from inadequacy and insecurity so that in fact it could more aptly be termed a gang. There are manifestations of this in the growing popularity of organised coach tours and holiday camps, where there is no need, or opportunity, for independent thought or action, and in the preference for living in any kind of suburban sprawl with its bingo club and so-called amenities, rather than in true country where personal resources and relationships are required of each individual. In spite of material advantages and communications undreamt of by our forebears, remote farms and hamlets all over the country are deserted, the specious attraction of noise and numbers having lured their former occupants into urban developments.

I am not suggesting that the imaginative faculties can only flourish in rural surroundings or that it is morally better to live in them. With a poor upbringing and education the country child or adult is as stunted in his imaginative development as any urban one, but for him the opportunities exist when or if he is able to benefit from them, while for the city-dweller today the factors of commercialised entertainment, speed, noise and overcrowding are all intensified. These destroy any sense of wonder – that ability to find, without rational understanding or justification, delight and surprise in all experiences. To deal successfully with the mechanics of urban life we have to believe that we are in full control of our material existence and that there is nothing rationally inexplicable which might influence or overtake us. We are preoccupied with traffic, parking systems and all kinds of instructions; we have to be quick in all that we do, while code numbers for telephone and postal addresses add to our already overburdened memories. We may think ourselves happy to live in this way, but all such information is unproductive and the attention we give to it absorbs the interest and energy which we could otherwise devote to imaginative efforts. These would make us both richer and more individual in our resources, our powers of expression and our contribution to our environment.

Increasing numbers have, or wish, to live in cities and we must find a way of making the most of urban benefits and of greater safety, hygiene and comfort without losing the richness of sensory effort and experience. We derive great material advantages from technological and scientific achievements, and it is tragic that we are so indiscriminate in our acceptance of these that we have not discovered how to use the health and leisure they offer to extend and develop our imaginative faculties.

We live in a time of inevitable collectivisation in which mass communications, mass media, and the mass of humanity itself constantly intrude upon our awareness and threaten to reduce the unique to a dull average. Yet the mass consists of individuals and its manifestations are the result of their accomplishment, and whatever the material achievements of our age, each one of us still needs to wonder, to create and to cherish our particular attributes. If we were encouraged in this by our education, we might transform the lumpish mass into a sentient constructive unity, but even to begin to realise this ideal, every teacher must realise the extent to which educational values and practices are determined both by sterile tradition as well as by commercial materialism, and he must free himself from their influence by rediscovering his own powers of imagination and consequently becoming an imaginative teacher.

5

The Influence of Contemporary Society on Educational Values and Practices

Educationists must assuredly struggle against conformism and must resist the imposition of all dogmatism, including their own.
SIR JULIAN HUXLEY: *Essays of a Humanist.*

IN every generation there are obstacles to sound and comprehensive education, and in the past these were the obvious and challenging ones of poverty and inadequate educational opportunities for the larger part of the population. The reformers of those times were perhaps fortunate in that they could clearly recognise the evils they had to combat, and although we still have some way to go in abolishing social injustice, decreasing the size of classes and replacing obsolete buildings, we are at least conscious of these shortcomings and we have to some extent overcome material inadequacies. Yet we are today faced with evils as great, though more subtle and insidious, because they derive from material prosperity – even from the efficiency of education itself – and are superficially attractive, popularly accepted and often difficult to identify. They are founded, I believe, in our misunderstanding and neglect of the imaginative faculties, and although this is not generally thought of as endangering or impoverishing our educational standards, it does in fact limit a child's full development as much as poor equipment or bad buildings. In fact some of the most imaginative teaching I have seen has been in old and overcrowded schools, perhaps partly

66

because in these there is a practical challenge to be faced and overcome.

Each age has its especial problems, and each makes to history its particular contribution through which a living tradition is created. Tradition is only dead and destructive to our development when in its name past conventions are thoughtlessly perpetuated and reproduced.

Every teacher should be gratefully conscious of outstanding achievements, both past and present, and he should integrate these into his experience and into that of his pupils. But he should also be clear-sighted in his estimate of the pervasive influence of his own education as well as that of contemporary society which, with its inevitable standardisation and tense insistence upon greater concentrations of humanity, greater speed and mechanical efficiency, shapes our lives and forms our values. He must relentlessly question everything which impinges upon a child's learning and experience, and at the same time accept nothing on the one hand because it is antique or traditional, or on the other because it is fashionable and a likely passport to wealth and power.

Admittedly this is a council of perfection, for to solve the problems of education today we have only the upbringing and background which have produced those problems. We have grown up with our education and in our society, we have been conditioned by them, we have contributed to them and strengthened their characteristics, and we cannot escape being partially blinded by their enveloping fog of habit and convention.

But we must attempt to understand the quality of our inheritance and the source and nature of our values, because otherwise we are teaching with prejudice instead of with perception.

First we can be thankful for the medical, scientific

and technical achievements which give a healthier and materially higher standard of life for every child, and which provide better physical conditions and equipment in schools where a far wider curriculum with more scope for experiment is therefore possible. We appreciate the extent of this progress when we read Harold Owen's account of his early schooling in the first volume of his biography of his brother Wilfred.

There is also the outstanding advance in educational thinking which has an interest in, and care for, individual accomplishment and which attempts to give each child the best education most suited to his particular aptitude. This is a hard-won ideal and one which we should always be ready to further and defend, for it is constantly threatened by considerations of efficiency and expediency which have no regard for manifestations of original sensibility and imagination.

This ideal is also threatened by the legacy of our own academic education with its almost absurd obsession with the factual aspect of rational thought and with assessable results. Man's intuitive awareness certainly existed before his mastery of factual deduction, and the conception of education as an extension of this awareness is older than the vitiated classical education which has for so long been predominant. From Plato to the present day philosophers and poets have emphasised that the intellect is but one specialised aspect of the self; that truth, imaginatively and emotionally experienced, is far more potent and profound than that which is only grasped rationally, and that it is useless, as well as positively harmful, to appeal to the logical understanding of a child while that understanding is still undeveloped. Our own education has made it difficult for us to believe in the truth of this and other advice; we cannot see how it could be carried out in everyday teaching, and so, in our effort to make education ever more rationally efficient, and whatever our protestations, we ignore imagination and the care for the individual which necessarily goes with it.

There is evidence of this in our acceptance of factual examination as the best method of measuring a child's achievement and progress. Undoubtedly it is the most practical and orderly, and the most easily understood by a generation whose imaginative understanding has had little chance to develop, but it takes no account of the manifold talents and abilities of which academic intelligence is but one. The quality and extent of the imaginative faculties are difficult, if not impossible, to examine, and so, although these are fundamental in a mature personality, we are apt, whether consciously or not, to discourage them. Our present form of education frequently falls short of catering for each individual child with his unique characteristics and gifts, for all children, whether or not possessing academic intelligence, are pushed through a curriculum based upon rational values and attainment which is popularly acclaimed as 'sound' or 'good'. Sad examples of this are in the introduction of external examinations for secondary modern school children, and the demand for a certain number of G.C.E. passes for students wishing to go to an art school or to undertake an unacademic career such as nursery nursing, in which creative imagination and understanding are of far greater importance than examinable reason.

A child of low academic ability often has considerable talent, understanding and powers of communication on a different level and in other directions, and these cannot be assessed by formal examination. Many such children would have been the Christ's Fools of medieval times, and even if they are backward in intellectual thought, the name testifies to their instinctive wisdom and dignity. Yet to support the popular ideal of efficiency and to add to statistical evidence (which assures us of our own competence but makes us forget the needs of individuals) these children have to take examinations which can do nothing but convince them of their own inadequacy. The argument that such examinations are purposely designed to be within the range of their low academic intelligence is a gratuitous insult both to the children and to enlightened teachers, while it merely demonstrates our own stupidity in being unable to appreciate anything but academic standards, however debased these may be. Worst of all, it persuades us to accept the vicious belief that, because factual knowledge and reasoning are all-important, a quick-witted child is 'better' than his slower companion.

The most cogent argument in favour of comprehensive schools is that in them the social distinctions between children of differing intellectual ability are lessened if not abolished. Yet I have heard of several where, because of the difficulties of accommodation, only those receiving prizes for academic successes are invited with their parents to the prize-giving. The less able, and their parents, are rejected, and are consequently subjected to discrimination greater than if they were segregated in a separate school.

Everyone needs as much rational understanding as he is capable of, and because it is necessary in the communication of logical ideas and in the understanding of argument, it must be encouraged by all possible means, especially by integrating it with the imaginative faculties. Yet to redress the imbalance in ourselves and in our society, and particularly for the sake of those to whom rational thought is difficult, we should remember that personality is more persuasive than argument (it is the personality, for example, rather than the academic qualifications which makes a great teacher); that we can communicate and convince through the visual arts and those of dance, music and drama, and that in earlier times and in other civilisations this was the usual practice. In our complex and mechanised society we can never wholly return to imaginative and sensory forms of expression and communication – that would be as absurd as suggesting telepathy as a substitute for the telephone – but we can give them more attention and importance than we do at present, starting in the schools where the curriculum itself would acquire greater significance and unity if the arts were respected as the expression and illumination of every age and country. How much more memorable, for instance, would the Eskimos be to a primary school child if he were familiar with their carving, or Russian history of the last hundred years to a secondary school one if it were brought to life through the literature and music of the time. Events in schools could be celebrated through the arts instead of by factual explanation, where as much recognition could be given to those who excel in creative imagination as to those who win scholarships for academic work, and where the importance of imaginative comprehension and relationships in every aspect of home and school life could be emphasised.

In spite of the work and example of many enlightened teachers, instruction still has pre-eminence over experience in far too many schools, and this rational bias encourages those teachers who, because of their imaginative limitations, transform the creative arts into analytical and critical exercises and the study of their history. Yet in any of the arts it is the impact of the whole work, and our experience of it, which is of primary importance, and while an understanding of the component parts may at some time add to our appreciation, fragmentary analysis and criticism can only result in that joyless academic knowledge which has for so long passed as culture. For his personal enrichment a child

71

should know of, and as far as possible grow up with, his aesthetic heritage, and according to his ability he should record and communicate his appreciation. But even if he cannot express it, his response to the whole work, which in its entirety communicates the creator's particular interest and achievement, is what profoundly influences his personality and development. All too often, especially in the higher classes of the secondary schools where a child is wrongly supposed no longer to be capable of creative work, the arts are presented in terms of factual criticism, so that we are in danger of becoming a nation of critics, able to expound and analyse, but impotent when creative imagination is required.

The popular Victorian attitude to art, that every picture tells a story, is not so far removed from us today, for we often hear discussed every possible aspect of a painting – metaphysical, philosophical, psychological and sociological – with scarcely a passing reference to its all-important visual impact. It would seem that we take every opportunity to escape the effort of a direct visual response, perhaps because it is easier for those with academic intelligence to spin words around a work of art than it is for them simply to look at it; in fact to give their attention to it with imaginative comprehension, to be receptive and to see without rational prejudice.

Our traditional forms of education promote word-spinning. At a recent education conference a university professor of classics is reported to have said: 'The test of culture is the power to converse intelligently and intelligibly with educated men in general', which is fair enough, but he went on to say how tiresome it had been for him to spend a day with an archaeologist who would only talk of his own subject. The professor might well have learnt something from his companion which would have extended his own awareness, and although courtesy undoubtedly demands that we are willing to talk about topics of general interest, there is a danger of accepting fluent conversation, already highly valued in this country, and sometimes degenerating into the merely glib, as a manifestation of culture. In this context A. N. Whitehead observes: 'A merely well-informed man is the most useless bore on God's earth.'

Depth of knowledge is more important than breadth, creation than criticism, and we must not allow facile reasoning to supplant imaginative effort and enquiry, for then we have no profound sensibility with which to recognise and combat bogus accomplishment. By reason alone we can only succeed in perpetuating sterile traditionalism, the ubiquitous neo-Georgian style in architecture, for example, or the official portraiture in each year's Royal Academy exhibition, which express nothing but our incapacity to create or enjoy anything which reflects the spirit of our own age.

Too great an emphasis on rational explanation denies us imaginative understanding. When a child is introduced to a painting, perhaps Botticelli's 'Birth of Venus', by an account of the story, or by an enumeration of the relevant dates, school, style and influences, he is likely for ever afterwards to see it in narrative or these incidental terms. Or when the New English translation of the New Testament was published, all the comment which I read was on its usefulness in factual clarification and information. But for me, and for millions like me who are not scholarly, the New Testament must stand as an all-embracing imaginative truth if it is not to fall into scraps of controversial detail which have no bearing upon our personal experience and are of concern only to theologians and scholars. The former translation was written in the great age of English literature when, with rich symbolism, language conveyed imaginative truth, and we have a far greater comprehension of any version of it if it is presented and considered as an imaginative unity. To rewrite and examine it in the chilly light of reason can only destroy its all-embracing significance.

Other instances of our preoccupation with facts in education can be found in the primary schools where the popularity of general knowledge tests requires a child to add to the considerable number of facts he must necessarily remember, such impermanent and unimportant ones as the names of cabinet ministers and of sportsmen, and where the emphasis on proven fact in his first instruction in mathematics and the sciences leads him to demand a rational explanation for everything. A young child's questions of: 'Is it true?' (scientifically) and 'What does it mean?' (rationally) to works of creative imagination are saddening because they reveal that he has lost his sense of wonder; mystery has become a problem which must be explained, and at an age when the rational and imaginative parts of his understanding should still be integrated he derides the existence of imaginative truth.

As well as trying to understand the influence of our education, both upon ourselves and our teaching methods, we should recognise that of the commercial materialism which permeates society today. Its values are comparable to those of dead traditionalism, for commerce welcomes those of quick wit who will conform to convention (whether antiquated or smartly fashionable) and discourages those of original interest and accomplishment. An individual capable of creative imagination and imaginative comprehension and understanding has the resources which enable him not only to recognise all aspects of quality, but which also give him an independent and enquiring mind with personal preferences and judgments. He will not accept every standardised idea and he is irritating to the public relations officer to whose steady stream of half-truths he will not respond.

In his address at the dedication of the Robert Frost Library, John Kennedy said: 'For art establishes the basic human truths which must serve as the touchstones of our judgment. The artist, however faithful to his personal vision of reality, becomes the last champion of the individual mind and sensibility against an intrusive society and an officious state.'

Today men with powers of facile reason but often of little integrity or principle are forming our tastes and habits, and there is a growing assumption that they not only can, but that they have the right to, manipulate the lives of those with lesser intellectual ability. The most carefully planned commercial onslaught is directed at such adults and children, and a public relations officer once boasted to me: 'There is nothing I cannot popularise and sell to those whose I.Q. is under 100.' So Christ's Fool becomes Mammon's Dupe, and the child who should reveal his simple wisdom, reflects instead the degrading vulgarity of our age, and the child in the E stream is indeed often, and tragically, 'worse' than his contemporary in the A.

As individual parents and teachers we deplore such cynical and repellent exploitation, but nevertheless we support it, both by our tolerance of certain sales techniques as well as by our teaching methods which encourage the quick-witted at the expense of the imaginative. When we try to educate those of limited academic intelligence we accept the wholly rational approach as inevitable, adjusting it to the stature of the so-called 'common man'. Fearing that a victim of commercial materialism will reject our efforts, we embellish these with cheap tricks and a flashy presentation, thus debasing them still further. In fact all we do is to reduce knowledge and experience to the trivial dimensions of a television advertisement, so that 'Common Man' is taught passively to depend upon second-hand and second-rate ideas and images, and to lose all confidence in his personal ability and accomplishment.

We forget that 'Common Man' has been created by the imbalance in man, for when there is a constructive relationship between the imaginative and the rational faculties no man can be said to be commoner than another, for each is unique and each knows the dignity of realising his particular achievement and through it of making his contribution to the community. Within the last two centuries we have arrived at the conscious degradation of Common Man, when his worst attributes of greed, stupidity and prejudice have been fostered in order to keep him 'common' so that he may serve Commercial Man's purpose. Neither the material nor the spiritual dimensions of the television advertisement are natural to Common Man: they are contrived for him while he is conditioned for them. This is not necessarily the result of an intentional and vicious wish to degrade others. We are all guilty in so far as we subscribe to social and educational values which are deeply rooted in materialism, which glorify the rational and destroy the imaginative.

If we play down to a child's rational limitations we are confining his development to an even more paltry form of our own understanding, whereas if we respect his dignity and acknowledge his potential as an imaginative being we give him the opportunity for limitless development.

To compete for, and to try to capture, the attention of the unsophisticated by methods which we would otherwise scorn, debases both the recipient and what we have to offer. It is an insult to his particular personality, for in giving anything, from a present to a child to the sharing of ideas and experiences and the imparting of information in teaching, there must never be any trickery, condescension or patronage but always the greatest respect. For this reason the 'Have Fun!' outfits and the 'How-To-Do-It' books are odious. They are commerce's direct attack on education, and from falsely assumed positions of superiority they offer second-hand ideas and shoddy materials already half-assembled, urging 'Have Fun' . . . drawing, painting, or whatever activity can be financially exploited. The most nonsensical advertisement for these which I have ever seen read: 'Have Fun! It's Quick! It's Easy! Embroidery Without A Needle!'.

In making every attempt to understand the general influences of our society, our part in furthering them and their effect upon our teaching methods and educational system, we must take account of the particular manifestations of speed, noise and the absence of solitude, which to a large extent determine our physical environment and therefore our values and the scope of our imaginative ability.

The pace of life today presses upon a child no less than upon an adult, and the emphasis on speed can be found in our measurement of success at every stage of his development – how soon can he walk, talk, read, write or pass examinations – in fact how much in quantity, rather than in quality, he knows and accomplishes. The able are urged to hurry on to do still more, while the slow must hasten to catch up. Of primary importance is the speedy acquisition of economically rewarding information and in some schools vocational specialisation starts as early as the age of 13, while the small amount of time alloted to the arts betrays the little respect there is for them. Instead of questioning the necessity for speed and trying to understand its implications, we allow every child to be swept into its whirlpool. Even at home his leisure is rarely tranquil;

one occupation swiftly supercedes another, while objects and toys are thoughtlessly acquired and swiftly discarded, so that he misses the contact with quality, both of material and of personal association, which characterises a long-owned and much-loved possession.

For the healthy growth and gradual maturing of his personality a child must have time to realise the nature and significance of his accumulated knowledge, to assimilate the whole of each experience instead of noting its isolated parts, and slowly and firmly to take root in his personal discoveries and relationships.

Because he needs time for the coherent integration of his intellect with his imagination, many a child is slow in discovering and developing his especial aptitude. If an intellectually able child is hurried through his school career he may well be successful in academic examinations, but such success will be only transitory and superficial for it will have no sure basis in his imaginative understanding, and he may never have the satisfaction of knowing his full capabilities. So we frequently witness the declining ability of the precocious child; the first to read and write and the most successful in early tests is not always, or even often, the most truly intelligent adult, for his education has not been sensitively adjusted, both in time and content, to his development.

We accept noise as carelessly as speed, and in the primary schools it is often equated with progressive education. A child is naturally exuberant and consequently noisy, and in many of his activities noise is right and inevitable. But it can be both hysterical and unnecessary, and it is tolerated, if not encouraged, by some teachers who believe it to be proof of their enlightened approach. I have been told: 'You will love – infant school; you can hardly hear yourself speak.' But neither teacher nor child is capable of creative thought or imagination in an overwhelming din, which more often than not is the result of nervous tension, while it certainly engenders it. With the continuous noise of traffic in the streets, radio and television in the home and jet aircraft in the air we should in the primary schools be creating quiet and an appreciation of its quality.

In a secondary school we expect a child to listen to poetry and music, to look at painting and sculpture and to benefit from such experience. But all that he is likely to have had in his earlier years is the clamour of street and home and, being accustomed to ceaseless sound, fleeting images and a general restlessness in his environment, he finds it difficult to give his attention to any of the arts, quietly, without tension and regardless of time.

On the grounds of economic viability the size of schools is increasing steadily and children are forced into greater crowds. Some may thrive in a school of 2,000, some are content in the smaller unit organised for them within the large, but many, and often the less intellectually able, are overwhelmed by the mass of humanity. On her first day at her new secondary school of 600, which today is considered reasonably small, an 11-year-old girl said she felt 'quite sick' because there were so many children at the morning assembly. Soon for such children there will be no smaller schools, and we should seriously question the legitimacy of educational arguments which emphasise economic factors at the expense of the human.

Solitude is neither advocated nor encouraged in education today, and in primary schools activities are sometimes relentlessly well organised. But throughout his life, at home and at school, a child should have as much encouragement in solitary play as he has at present in group activity. As well as being physically energetic and gregarious, a child is contemplative and creative, but before he has time to resolve these characteristics so that they are a fundamental and well-balanced part of his personality, he is caught up in the social involvement of the nursery or infant school class, where if he prefers to play alone he is likely to be labelled abnormal. It is important for every child to be able to co-operate with others within a group, for personal relationships are for most of us the basis of living, but it is equally important for him to be independent and alone, serene and receptive to all the sensory impressions he receives from animate and inanimate creation. His imaginative comprehension and response are dulled and finally destroyed if he is always striving to assert himself or having to submit to the demands of other children in a group, which with no creative purpose readily deteriorates into a gang. In fact it is in a gang that he may seek security in adolescence and later life if we have not helped him in his early years to occupy himself in solitude.

Even his time for free activity rarely gives a young child opportunity for contemplation. When up to forty-five other infants are pursuing their chosen occupations, the calm necessary for creative imagination is naturally unattainable, and teacher and child alike come to accept in the name of art any casual cutting, hammering, scribbling or dabbling with paint. Orderly teaching is regarded as essential if a child is to progress in academic learning (careful thought is given, for example, to the techniques of teaching a child to read) and it is no less necessary if, from the earliest age, he is to develop in and through the visual arts. Indeed because so much more time and attention are given to the teaching of the academic subjects, a child is convinced that these are the only ones worthy of serious consideration, so that even if it is in the visual arts that he is likely to excel, he believes that his gifts are worthless in the real business of making his way in life.

In the last sixty years fashion in the up-bringing of a child has swung from one extreme to another, in each case to the detriment of his just development and experience. At the beginning of the century many a child of conscientious parents was brought up in complete isolation from any other outside his own family, often not in constructive solitude but in sterile loneliness, while today it is difficult for him to escape from the tumult of community life. We must now find a constructive balance between group activities and solitude so that a child has the opportunity to realise every aspect of his personality.

These conditions I have described are, I believe, some of the ways in which the values of our society and education are faithfully reflected in our teaching methods. If we are successfully to educate the imagination of every child we should beware of them, recognising as clearly as the reformers in the past the dangers which beset our educational system and policies, and realising the truth of William Wash's statement in *The Use of Imagination*: 'Meanness of understanding, ugliness of milieu, the attitudes of the robot, these are the characteristics of an age suffering from an anaemia of the imagination, the organ most vividly and ultimately concerned with life.'

6

Imaginative Teaching

If the intellect measures all worth with the yardstick of its own creation, the intuition takes no measurement at all. It knows that all life is one, yet separate, and that all forms of life have equal validity. It moves serene with certainty and therefore tolerant of all that lives.

CHRISTMAS HUMPHREYS: *Zen Buddhism.*

To educate the imagination we must teach imaginatively, and if the results of our teaching are to be creative our methods must be creative. This implies, as in any other effort of creative imagination, an interrelationship of rational knowledge with imaginative comprehension and understanding.

As a young teacher I was haunted by the old jibe: 'Those who can't, teach', for I was conscious that my own work was undistinguished, and yet I sensed that teaching is as creative an art as any other. Now I believe that while knowledge, as profound as possible, of a teacher's own subject is essential, his personal accomplishment in it is not, and that my own lack of it in fact helped me. From my art school training I was fortunate in having a background of experience and appreciation, I knew the difficulties and problems in the practice of art and some of the crafts, I never wanted a child to work in my way for I knew this to be of little worth, and because I had an exuberant interest in people as well as a considerable visual curiosity, I welcomed the diversity of personality and achievement in my classes. This carried me through the early years of instinctive teaching which slowly and surely developed my own awareness and enabled me consciously to form my beliefs.

From my experience I am convinced that as soon as it is more than a mere imparting of facts within a framework of regimented discipline, teaching is indeed a creative art which demands imagination. A teacher must have imaginative comprehension and understanding of the especial talents and potential of every child as well as of the fundamentals (and not only the current manifestations) of his subject, which is the medium for his work. From his subject he selects factors and qualities which he believes will extend the awareness of each child, and this extension is his creative achievement. But it is not a finite work which can be displayed or assessed, and the result cannot be anticipated, for it depends upon the co-operation, will and initiative of another unique human being. As well as never knowing exactly what form the result of his teaching will take, neither can a teacher know when it will appear. He may see a result immediately or at some time during a child's school career, but he may well never know what he has achieved. This is his leap in the dark and his exploration beyond the security of certain facts and results, for he teaches with the conviction that it is only in his own time and in his own way that a child will, from the efforts and disciplines essential to the subject, produce original work which will be significant in his development.

Especially for those who are outstandingly accomplished in their own subject, this is perhaps the most difficult part of imaginative teaching, for it gives a teacher none of the satisfaction of propagating his own interests or of obtaining an immediate and acclaimed result. Instead he is required to give his disinterested attention both to his subject and to each child, genuinely welcoming personal, often surprising, work.

For the nourishment of his own creative imagination a teacher should be fully of his time, enjoying its achievements and recognising its failings, possessing in fact an imaginative understanding of it which he must relate both to the disciplines of his subject and to the needs of the children in his charge.

In this he should try to be objective: he does not have to identify himself absolutely with all the characteristics of the era, and the teacher who adopts self-consciously the most fashionable manifestation of his subject and the habits and beliefs of his pupils is of little help to them. Such a teacher has an immature fear of acknowledging differences in age and outlook and of accepting his responsibility of exercising adult discernment. No child benefits from contact with an unresolved personality, but he is enriched by the considered ideas and experience of individuals of different generations.

On the other hand a teacher may repudiate his society, having only nostalgia for the past, disparagement of the present and pessimism about the future. This carping attitude has formerly been characteristic of many a scholarly teacher who has relied upon erudition and reason alone and whose education has not prepared him to live wholeheartedly in the present, accepting its demands and challenge. But although he may fancy that he belongs in spirit to an earlier, and in his opinion superior, age, he is no less part of his own time, for the nature of his rejection of it is determined by certain aspects which he fears. From these, and from the children who represent them, he retreats into the security of expert academic teaching and a glorification of by-gone customs and creeds. He is knowledgeable when he is dealing with any historical event but he blusters aggressively when he is faced with an original work, situation or personality. To a limited extent he can help the potential scholar, but never the academically slower child, for to him imagination is suspect and he destroys it in its infancy, while all that he encourages, even in the intellectual child, is an arid traditionalism.

The work of each generation of teachers reflects the characteristics of their time, and as there are great and popular artists, so are there great and popular teachers. Each is the product of his generation, but the great teacher questions and discriminates. He is aware of the essential qualities both in his society and in his subject, he realises the needs of each child and, because these are his first concern, he uses his subject to help the child on his way to maturity rather than to propagate his own preferences. His creative imagination and imaginative understanding takes his teaching out of the confines of his particular era and, while he gives every child the opportunity for individual appreciation and accomplishment unimpeded by convention, he is also an inspiration to succeeding generations.

Most of us are popular teachers, the significance of our work being determined by our response to the general influences and opinions of our age. Every teacher should beware, however, of becoming dominated by these, for then, like the immature escapist I have described, his imaginative understanding is limited and instead of questioning a prevailing fashion, he confidently allows his enthusiasm for it to override his interest in the unique and unpredictable development of every child.

Any able teacher can produce from a reasonably able child a certain result and it is always tempting to make sure of a fashionable one. In the visual arts it is as easy today to condition a young child so that he paints an example of naïve child art, or an older one an expressionist or abstract picture, as it was thirty years ago to teach theoretical perspective which resulted in neatly correct drawings of cubes and cones or buckets and brooms.

In every case the teacher plans and dominates the entire process. He is sincere, but he intends, unimaginatively, to obtain a predetermined result. He is apt to misinterpret the work of a great teacher, so that in the past Froebel's Gifts, sensitively contrived for a child's apprehension of unity and order, degenerated into mechanical exercises, Cizek's creative teaching into do-as-you-please Free Art, Paul Klee's imaginative idea of taking a line for a walk into crude crazy-paving patterns, while the teacher's own methods soon become historical evidence of the eccentricities of a certain time. The more efficient he is, the more he inhibits personal imagination, for from him a child acquires an inflexible idiom and scale of values which, if he is to become a creative member of his own generation, he will later have consciously to reject.

The most unfortunate teacher is he whose conformity to wholly rational considerations makes him fear that unless he dictates the exact method of starting, continuing and finishing the work, a child will never achieve what he believes to be a satisfactory result. At best he is trying to ensure that the child will not miss an essential experience, but at worst he wants nothing other than a standardised result and to avoid making any imaginative effort himself. In the visual arts he is undismayed by the reproduction, often approximate, of some commonplace image, perhaps drawn by himself on the blackboard for the children to copy, and he has the attitude of the teacher who told me: 'Teaching is like the recipe for a good pudding. Once you know how to do it, you just keep on with it.'

This attitude is the mainstay of the how-to-do-it books and have-fun outfits, which undoubtedly fascinate a child because they are especially designed to give him a spurious sense of achievement, enabling him with little effort to reproduce something which will be applauded because it conforms to an accepted pattern. But the arbitrary rules and techniques destroy his confidence in his own powers of observation and imagination and they eliminate any possibility of personal experience. His superficial enjoyment is no reason why these travesties of art and craft should be encouraged, any more than his liking for iced lollies justifies an unrelieved diet of them.

Once and for all we should reject this approach as well as the commercialised recipes, for the teacher who anticipates a result paralyses each child with his own prejudices and imparts false values which are a denial of creative teaching, while no subject can ever be fun in the frivolous sense of the word. Each involves individual initiative, choice and concentrated attention, and the only assurance of enjoyment which we can honestly offer is that deep satisfaction which comes from persisting in these efforts and in trying to achieve something which seems always to be just beyond our grasp.

At the other extreme from the recipe method is the kindly teacher who is unwilling to acknowledge the true characteristics of society and the pressure upon every child of crude, often cruel, commercialism. He takes refuge in an often extravagant interpretation of free expression and free discipline, and when such teaching is practised with so much good will it is hard to say that it makes nonsense of education, and that it is the cause of the disillusionment of many a young teacher who finds the idealism of his college education lectures useless when he is trying to organise a class of forty riotous primary school children, so that they work purposefully and without unnecessary mess and destruction. But I believe this to be the case, for numerous recently qualified teachers have come to me in despair about the chaos in their art and craft classes, and for a lecturer or teacher to ignore realities, however commonplace or unpleasant, is to withhold help from both the child and the student who work in the context of contemporary conditions.

An infant school teacher or an education lecturer is apt to claim that a young child has infinite powers of spontaneous imagination and creativity, which, without guidance or influence, will emerge as a matter of course. In a book on primary school teaching, recently recommended to students, I read that it is now commonly acknowledged by both parents and teachers that children can play, draw, paint and use constructive materials without instruction, and that it is unnecessary to offer a subject to young children who have something to say and know the way in which to say it.

The teaching of a young child, and indeed a child of any age, must of course be sensitively related, both in content and in the amount of direction, to his ability and personality. But although the conception of every child as an unspoiled and imaginatively creative primitive is a lofty ideal and reassuring to all of us who long for a better society, it is in fact far removed from the reality of the child who, satiated with an over-abundance of toys and trivial occupations, complains: 'I don't know what to do', who falls asleep at school because he has been up too late watching television or roaming the streets, who may be more likely to destroy than to construct, whose visual experience is limited to comics and advertisements, and who has probably lost his spontaneity, confidence and sensibility either through his wretched environment or his pretentiously genteel upbringing.

When in the early 1940s I started to teach in state schools, undernourished, illclad and dirty children were not uncommon. They were materially deprived, and

88

their primitive idiom and interest were untouched by commercialised sophistication. They brought their robust pavement drawings into the art class where their enthusiasm was largely because they had never before had the chance to mix colour, to find out what they could do with pencil, pen or crayon, or what they could make out of clay or wood. They looked and worked intently because there were few other such enjoyable occupations in their lives. No one can possibly regret that those days of poverty are past, but we can regret that because we have not related our teaching methods to the realities of social conditions we have missed the opportunity of giving every child an imaginative enrichment which is as great as the material. The lively wall and pavement drawings have disappeared, and we have allowed factual and commercial considerations to dominate the life of every child and to force him into conformity and pseudo-sophistication at an ever earlier age, so that he is well on the way to being as imaginatively deprived as formerly he was materially.

We must accept every child as he is and not as we would wish him to be. We do not help him by romancing over him, and we strengthen his preference for purposeless pastimes if our teaching methods are irrelevant to his personal experience and needs. Before they were translated into an often sentimental form, the original theories of free expression and free discipline made an immense and valuable contribution to educational thought and practice. But they are not the final answer for all time and in most subjects they have long been disassociated from mere laissez-faire. Yet this interpretation still persists in the teaching of the visual arts, especially in the primary schools, and in their name a teacher will ignore the essential discipline and experience of the subject, leaving each child without guidance or suggestion to do as he pleases, so that neither he nor the teacher has any sense of imaginative purpose.

As soon as a teacher, with whatever good intentions, abandons his responsibility of providing a framework of effort and activity for his subject, some other factor will take his place. Today commerce intervenes, and a child, accustomed at home to comics, have-fun and how-to-do-it sets, will attempt to reproduce the grotesque images he has been persuaded to admire. His expression is not free or personal; it is resolved by alien and often shoddy influences, and in it there is no trace of his innate sensibility and awareness which the exponents of freedom intend to encourage.

We must know what we mean by freedom. Not one of us, even as an infant, is free as an innocent child of nature, for every society establishes conventions of behaviour and belief which from the earliest age determine the physical habits, the rational thought and the imaginative ability of every individual. The way in which a baby is fed, clothed and handled has a profound effect upon his early development, while later the interests of his family and the customs of his locality influence his understanding. To have as adults any degree of freedom, we must be aware of these established influences and cultivate the imaginative understanding which will enable us to be independent of the pernicious and consciously to select those most beneficial for our own development. By an equally conscious selection of experiences inherent in each subject, and by a thoughtful presentation of them we must as teachers try to ensure that every child is capable of a similar, if not greater, imaginative understanding.

In education free-discipline is self-discipline. A child is not free if he is aimless or destructive, for then he is at the mercy of his impulses. When, however, he can to some extent control and organise himself and his activities in relation to others and to his environment, he begins to comprehend freedom, for he is free from the inhibitions of personal insecurity and the frustrations of incompetence.

With an imaginative approach to both the child and the subject, it is possible to educate him in this self- and free-discipline, neither imposing an adult form nor leaving him defenceless before the onslaught of commercial influences. He may apparently enjoy and benefit from an imposed discipline and the consequent achievement of a standardised result, but this will have had little significant effect upon his development, because through his own initiative he will have learnt nothing which will add to his awareness and give him the resources to deal sensitively and creatively with subsequent problems and situations. He must be put in the way of the disciplines which are inherent in any creative work, and while the effort and achievement must be his own, he needs adult stimulus and suggestion. His final freedom will be in his personally controlled and organised creative imagination and in his imaginative relationships with everybody and everything around him.

With an imaginative relationship between him and the teacher, a child acquires the assurance which enables him to work out his ideas in his own, often unorthodox, way. The teacher respects each child's individuality; he welcomes his unique interests and his expression of them. In the visual arts he encourages him in intent observation which, as I shall explain in the next chapter, is the basis of his sensibility and development. Blake wrote: 'Every Eye sees differently. As the Eye, such the Object,' and each child notices and enjoys a different aspect of an object and of his environment, while he reacts differently to forms, colours and tones – one likes a large flowing form, another a small jagged shape, one finds a dark colour exciting, to another it is gloomy. Through gradually becoming conscious of his personal vision and preferences he is released from the conformity which presses in upon him from every side, and the outcome is his free expression, untrammelled by adult conventions, of his deeply felt response to any experience.

This expression must be integrated with his self-discipline, for to be able to express his ideas a child must be free from the paralysing encroachment of muddle; he must be able coherently to organise both the chosen aspect of his subject as well as the medium in which he will recreate it. Only the especially gifted child is capable of doing this on his own initiative. The others will need wise adult help, about which I will say more in the next chapter, for left to himself the inept child will repeat interminably, and often hopelessly, the same formalised image or chaotic mess, while the able will reproduce, also interminably, impersonal ideas derived from commercial sources. In neither case is this free, personal, and imaginative expression.

If when he is young we do not offset the often deplorable aesthetic and spiritual conditions in a child's daily life, giving him by imaginative teaching personal imaginative experience and the confidence both to express it in his own way and to recognise and enjoy it in the work of others, we should not be cynical or dismayed when shoddy trivialities form his tastes and habits and transform him in to an unco-operative adolescent.

This is not to say that I would wish to rear a child in a hot-house of refined aesthetic sensibility, and if I were to attempt it I would fail, for either a child would reasonably, and rightly, rebel against the standards I would be imposing upon him, or he would accept them and grow up divorced from the values and opinions of his own generation and unable to adjust himself to them. A profusion of excellence can overwhelm a child, and each has to live in the world as it is, coming to terms with it by knowing for himself its best and worst aspects. He does not have to accept every manifestation of his society but neither has he absolutely to reject it, and if in our teaching we can find a happy mean between the extremes of an imposed discipline and of licence, so that we preserve and develop his imaginative faculties and give him a truer sense of values, he will be the more successful both in his own life and in creating a wholesome society.

The experience required for the full and balanced education of every child can be found in his daily life and in the particular qualities of each subject in his school curriculum. A child may need help in recognising the comparative worth of his experiences – that, for instance, it is more informative and memorable to study for himself the growth of an insect than to watch it on television. The necessary experiences are simple and direct, a part of everyday life and learning, and apparently commonplace to a teacher who enjoys a flamboyant gesture and wants a startling result, while the child himself may only dimly realise their significance. But they extend his sensory and intellectual awareness, they become part of his sensibility and they are resources which he can draw upon for his work of creative imagination.

The following is a list of 'things I remember' and 'things I like' supplied by children of ages ranging from 8-15: the smell of damp in sheds and cellars, of hot pennies, bacon frying, geranium leaves, an empty classroom; the feel of foam rubber, a cat's tongue, slippery seaweed, the hot wind in the underground; the colour of a cut beetroot, of my dog's eyes, orange paint, reflections in a shiny black car; the taste of ink, lemon peel, dandelion leaves, chalkiness in some medicines; the sound of a Salvation Army band, the squeak of the wheel in a hamster's cage, sparrows in the early morning; digging a very deep hole, crossing a river in a ferry boat, seeing the dinosaurs in the Natural History Museum.

We must make sure that every child has the time to be aware of, and receptive to, such experiences, that the hustle of his material existence does not make him forget them, and that we do not add to the super-abundance of his half-realised experience unnecessary ones which because of their complexity he cannot assimilate. In scale and speed all should be related to his capacity, and while, for instance, it is both important and valuable for a child to visit museums, art galleries and historical buildings in central London, we should not make him do and see too much or expect him to regurgitate every fact of his visit on his return to school. Nor should we be irritated if his recollections are seemingly trivial; when a young child goes to the Tower of London he may have a more vivid impression of the colour and smell of the river mud than of the Crown Jewels, for he may be like the child who, at the age of seven, was taken on an expediton to Caernarvon Castle and the splendour of the Welsh coast and has always referred to it as 'the day we saw the dead dog by the roadside'.

If education is to be truly constructive it can only progress, slowly and unpretentiously, at each child's rate of sensory and mental growth, and we must be content to provide him with a breadth of common experience, realising that the particular, which makes a decisive contribution to his personality, will only be significant to him when he is already familiar with the common. The profound and formative experience will emerge at an unpredictable time and from an unpredictable source, and the best we can do is to counteract the standardised, and imaginatively deadening, influences in a child's daily life by putting him in the way of simple efforts and disciplines so that by these he is prepared to benefit from a great experience whenever it may come in to his life. The thorough exploration by a child of a limited aspect of his environment is therefore a more certain help to him than a grandiose project intended to impart tremendous experience – in fact the fairy tale truth of the crock of gold in his back garden.

The foremost consideration in education is the wellbeing of every child and this is of far greater importance than the teacher's aggrandisement or that of his subject. When pride of place is given to the subject it is immediately rendered ineffectual as a means of education, for only the exceptionally gifted child will be able to surmount the rigid barrier of formal facts and reasoning, or the acquisition of a prescribed technique, and to develop his own understanding and form of expression. Teaching must be based upon human rather than doctrinaire considerations, and a teacher should always be ready to adapt a different aspect of his subject to meet the needs of a particular child, whose imaginative relationship with, an interpretation of it, forms the basis of his education. In his preoccupaton with his own interests the highly qualified specialist sometimes finds such adaptation difficult, and for this reason the best teacher is he whose human sympathy is as great, if not greater, than his academic qualifications. But when a subject is used in this way it is not debased; in fact its value and meaning are enhanced because on every level it is opened to individual interpretation and freed from the sterility of exclusive scholarship. Language, for example, is a weaker means of communication when it is limited to academic forms and unenriched by popular idiom, and the visual arts are continually revitalised by the use of new materials and, in recent decades, by the work of children, by popular art and by many aspects of technology.

Yet we do not teach by careful thought and planning alone, however sensitively these may be attuned to the needs of the individual child. We teach with our whole personalities, by the pervasive influence of our values and the quality and extent of our imagination. The greater the teacher's compassion and imaginative understanding, and the more surely based his values, the more successfully will he create a sympathetic relationship with his class and develop the imaginative faculties of every child in it. This in its turn will still further extend his own awareness and give him greater maturity.

Inevitably a teacher influences each child who will react for or against his personality and beliefs. We must acknowledge and accept the responsibility of our influence, neither evading nor overemphasising it, but endeavouring to make it constructive and realising that it is a necessary part of being a fully adult teacher. We should not be afraid to admit that we are in a position of authority, yet this is not one of coercive authoritarianism, but one in which, because of our more mature understanding and imagination, a child turns naturally to us for advice and help.

There can be no recipe for imaginative teaching, which, like any other creative art, is apparently simple in its unity of purpose and result. But this simplicity is deceptive and can only be achieved with imaginative understanding, possessed naturally by some instinctive teachers and acquired by others only after considerable experience and effort. Every teacher has his particular gifts and interests and he is himself continuously developing, while at the same time he is involved in an infinity of human situations in which each personality and problem is unique. He must give his full attention to the characteristics and potential both of his subject and also of every child, ensuring that each has first-hand experience, and that encouragement and recognition are given to his particular ability and achievement for the realisation of which he has the necessary time, quiet and solitude. Then to some extent the teacher must withdraw, perhaps never seeing any actual result of his work which, slowly but surely, will be nurturing the imaginative growth of every individual. But he will have the satisfaction of releasing creative energy, and of developing in each child, whatever his academic ability, that awareness which I believe to be the essence of educated man and the only possible basis of a civilised future.

7

The Education of Imagination

All is unity; all rests in unity, starts from unity, strives and leads towards unity and returns in to unity.

FRIEDRICH FROEBEL (1782-1852): *On Education*.

I F we are successfully to develop the imaginative faculties of every child, we must not only create in the schools an atmosphere and environment which reflects the best of contemporary life, but we must also have a clear understanding of the characteristics peculiar to each subject and its possible contribution to this aspect of education.

Through the study and practice of a subject a child should gain the experience essential to it. A genius will develop irrespective of his upbringing and environment, but for most of us the fertility of our imagination and the quality of all our achievement depend upon the variety and depth of our personal understanding in every part of life and education. Nothing is more shortsighted than early specialisation or the segregation of children of particular ability, for each child needs breadth of experience and every subject and every personality complements another. We can never foretell how, when or why a child will acquire fruitful knowledge, and if, in an attempt to hasten the course of his attainment, we deny him certain aspects of education or isolate him with others of comparable ability, we may in fact severely limit him. The child of 15, for instance, whose intellectual faculties have been intensely cultivated at the expense of his imaginative, is already committed to a stunted and one-sided existence in which he will never realise his full capabilities.

In terms of time and emphasis there must be a just balance between the claims of each subject; none must be given priority because it is currently fashionable or economically rewarding, for, to quote again from Sir Julian Huxley's *Essays of a Humanist*: 'in a properly unified curriculum separate studies will not compete for prestige and place, but can reinforce one another.' Each subject should in fact be studied or practised with regard to its inherent discipline and with as great a degree of excellence as each child can achieve at his particular stage of development, for this, rather than consciously correlated subjects or fabricated projects, gives him comprehension of value and realisation of the essential unity inherent in learning and understanding.

In a primary school art and craft are often considered only as adjuncts to another subject or to a project. A child draws to illustrate history or geography, he paints pictures and models figures and animals for a term-long study of another country, and although this is an admirable integration of his interests and skills, he nevertheless misses, in depth, the particular experiences which are to be found when the visual arts are practised for their own sake.

There is a fundamental difference in the educative purpose and effect between subjects in which an agreed result can legitimately be expected, and those in which we should never anticipate the form of the result and in which we welcome personal interpretation and idiom.

In one group of subjects, which includes mathematics and the sciences at any but research level, personal interpretation is impossible. The child or student must acquire some method of reasoning which will enable him to arrive at an unconditional conclusion. The method may involve intuitive comprehension or imaginative understanding, and it will necessarily give the child personal experience, but the predetermined result is inescapable. In another group – languages, history, geography, music and gymnastics – he has to acquire skills and learn to reproduce acknowledged facts, sounds or movements which he can then use in his own way and for his own purposes, while, in the expressive subjects – creative music, poetry and prose, dance, drama and the visual arts – the only techniques he must master are those necessary to the control and manipulation of his medium through which he can discover and develop his personal form of expression. The media in these subjects are sounds, words, his own physical movements and the materials of the visual artist or craftsman.

The first group of subjects is foremost in the promotion of rational and deductive thought, the second factual and associative, while the third is primarily concerned with the imagination. All three groups are inter-related, for imagination is inherent in mathematics and the sciences and some degree of rational thought in the arts, and experience in one group is likely to stimulate effort and accomplishment in another. For a young child, and well-educated older one, there can, and should be, a fusion in the experience which he derives from all his education; he will solve a mathematical problem with imagination as well as with intellectual reason, while in the arts his rational understanding will bring order to his sensibility and creative imagination. But I believe that basically these groups possess different educational disciplines and that it is reasonable, and I hope helpful, to differentiate between them.

It is important to remember that imagination is not limited to its usual association with aesthetic activity, nor rational thought with the academic subjects, and that both are essential in any creative achievement. Imagination is certainly necessary in mathematics and the sciences, for it is the faculty which enables us to explore beyond the confines of our certain knowledge and understanding and to relate facts and experiences so that we arrive at a conclusion which we have not wholly anticipated and have never before fully realised. Scientific discovery demands creative imagination, but, unlike a work of art, it does not necessarily stimulate and extend imagination in an observer. I accept, for instance, the existence of the telephone and of television and I am amazed that such means of communication should have been perfected, but neither, in its own right as a scientific discovery, inspires me to creative achievement or gives me greater imaginative understanding or experience.

Whatever is created or achieved in the sciences stands as an objective fact or belief, which may sooner or later be disproved. The fact, for example, that hot air rises was at one time discovered and we now accept it without question. Fifty years ago we also accepted the belief that the atom is the smallest indivisible particle of matter, which we now know to be untrue. But however permanent or impermanent the discovery, it exists in its own right; it does not mark a stage in the growth of the scientist's perception, and as his personality matures he does not inevitably produce work of greater significance. His achievement may as well be the outcome of youthful intelligence and initiative as of deepening awareness and personal maturity, and many scientific discoveries are in fact made by young men near the beginning of their careers. Nevertheless, whatever his age, a scientist's work is no less the product of his imaginative faculties functioning in his own time than that of any other scholar or artist, but for posterity his actual achievement is independent both of himself and his era, for it tells us nothing of his personality or of the characteristics of society and his response to them. We know, for instance, that Sir Alexander Fleming, from his observation, patience and imaginative understanding, discovered penicillin, but from that fact and from the benefit we derive from it, we know no more of him as an individual or of the decade in which he made this important discovery.

Imagination is more obviously and immediately present in the second group of subjects – the social studies, language and music – for it is not only necessary to any achievement in them, but imaginative comprehension and understanding are needed for their appreciation. At the same time the individuality of the scholar or creator, as well as the characteristics of the age in which he lives, are communicated by the completed work: a Victorian historian, for example, presents in a different idiom a different aspect of his subject than the historian of today, while we should never expect 18th century music to be indistinguishable from that of our own period.

Yet these subjects are bound up with facts, exact theories and techniques which, although they may be a constructive challenge for an able child and adult, are for the unintellectual an intrusion between him and his appreciation and understanding, creating a barrier which discourages him from further effort, while even the skills which the able child acquires can, if they are overemphasised, inhibit his imagination.

Evidence of these two facts can be found in musical education, in which the unacademic child is prevented from full participation because of his inability to master notation and theory, while in teaching art to children especially gifted in music, I have noticed that it is difficult for them confidently to experiment with their media, to express through it a personally observed aspect of their subject and in fact to exercise their creative imagination. In music they are used to working within the framework of a certain technique to achieve their own interpretation of an acknowledged form, and in the visual arts they are at first intimidated by having to rely upon their own resources without the support of definite rules and a certain result.

Any accomplishment in the third group – the expressive subjects – communicates the creator's response to his theme and to his medium as well as his personality in relation to his environment. As in the sciences, his work exists in its own right, and it has an objective form, meaning or purpose – a poem or a portrait, for example. But inevitably, and in common with the second group of subjects, it is also witness to the creator's characteristics and to those of his time. Landscape paintings by Claude, Constable and Cézanne reveal each man's visual interest and imagination, but these are in the context of the 18th, 19th and 20th centuries and they belong almost as much to the age as to the painter himself, while the work of a student or child can usually be identified as belonging to a particular era. An exception is an infant's painting, or that of an academically backward child, for this is independent of contemporary influences of which the painters are as yet unaware, and through the primitive symbolism it reveals only the sensibility and interest of the individual.

The artist makes a personal statement and, in the fact of its existence and whether or not it is his intention, he communicates with another personality and stimulates his imaginative faculties. As he matures, so his work matures, each example marking a stage in his development and betraying the extent and quality of his imagination. His achievement cannot factually be disproved or superceded, for we can never say that a work of art is 'right' or 'wrong'. We can only say that we prefer one to another, and this has more or less significance to us, according to the maturity of the artist as well as to that of our imaginative comprehension which reflects contemporary opinions and sensibility. In one age a Raphael Madonna will be considered pre-eminent in religious painting, in another an early Italian, but neither is proved better or worse by our preference within the popular judgment of our time.

The arts are unfettered by academic considerations, and in them factual knowledge, which might for some preclude participation and enjoyment, is of secondary importance. They thrive and have their being in imagination, being rooted in creative imagination and demanding for their appreciation an imaginative response, so that we can identify ourselves with the whole sum of experience and sensibility which is present in the work and through it we can develop in perception and understanding.

We learn and mature through personal experience, and although some degree of imagination is needed in the proper study and practice of all subjects, every aspect of it is required in the arts, and it is through them that we can most successfully rediscover, preserve and educate the imaginative faculties.

In education every one of the arts is important because each relates to a particular part of sensory awareness and consequent imagination. Music, and to some extent literature are concerned with the aural; sculpture and modelling with the spatial; these and many of the crafts with the tactile and the visual, to which painting and drawing are primarily related. Each of the arts develops and contributes to a different facet of the imagination, and we must understand the potential of our own subject in this aspect of education, because it is only through the imaginative teaching of every one that we can bring to the service of each child the richness and variety of both the physical world and of the arts.

Although he may not immediately or obviously benefit from it, every child should have experience in each of the arts. This will extend his general awareness and resources, while according to his particular talents, inheritance and environment he will most potently learn and develop through the one or two to which he is most responsive.

My concern is with the importance of the visual arts in the education of every child's imaginative faculties. Whether his particular gift is in academic, physical, social or aesthetic achievement I believe that each needs the practice of art and craft for his full and balanced development, and that in one branch or another every one can produce work of considerable quality, satisfying both to himself and to an observer. Although I would never give priority to the popular aims of art teaching – the provision of vocational skill or the production of greater aesthetic discrimination – I find that these often follow as a matter of course when I am giving my full attention to the development of individual visual awareness. As I have explained, imaginative understanding must precede rational analysis and criticism if these are to be constructive, and in art education, if skill and discrimination are to be, instead of mere embellishments, a significant and integrated part of an individual's endeavour and personality, they must be the outcome of creative imagination and imaginative comprehension and understanding.

If he is to develop the imaginative faculties, an art teacher must concentrate on what is in fact his job: the education of the visual, spatial and tactile senses through the disciplines and achievements which are implicit in an original work of art, just as the teacher of another subject must give his attention to the qualities essential to that.

The art teacher may have wider interests in, perhaps, literature or psychology, but he should never allow experiences peculiar to these to impinge upon those of the

visual arts which make their especial contribution to
sensory awareness. In my childhood it was fashionable
to emphasise the narrative content of a picture and of
picture-making, and in recent years many an art teacher
has not only interpreted a child's paintings and drawings
in psychological terms but has encouraged him to produce work of psychological significance. Both of these
approaches are legitimate, the one for the illustration
of literature and social studies and the other for the
professional psychiatrist, but in either case the child's
attention is drawn to descriptive or emotive subject
matter and diverted from the full exploration of colour,
tone and line and from discovering how he can use
them. This should be the purpose of an art class; a
narrative or descriptive subject may well be necessary
as a stimulus and vehicle for a child's exploration and
discovery, and undoubtedly there will be a psychological
aspect to his completed work, but the art teacher should
ensure that each child has the greatest and most direct
visual experience, and that other considerations are
kept in their proper place.

In the intent awareness of objects and related objects,
both natural and man-made, which is necessary for the
creation of an original work of art, the fundamental
effort is observation, and the more sensitive and acute
this is, the greater the significance and maturity of the
artist's work. He may be concerned with two- or three-
dimensional design, with representational or with
abstract drawing and painting, but whatever his idiom,
it derives from, and is inspired by, forms, colours, tones
and surfaces which he has directly or at some time
observed. He does not merely record; he gives his attention to all that he sees or has ever seen, observing qualities and characteristics which in time and by the
processes of his imagination he uses for his particular
purpose. He may be embodying in his work his

emotional, religious or sociological preoccupations, but inevitably his expression of them is in visual terms which give actual form to his intention and which communicate to an observer.

An artist or craftsman can only express his interest through a medium which is external to himself and which he has to select with a sensitive regard for its own characteristics and in relation to those of his subject. If he can sympathetically exploit his medium, handling it with an understanding of its particular nature rather than imposing upon it a rigid technique, his work will be immeasurably more lively and communicative, for his vivid experience will be externalised by his equally vivid expression of it in these terms.

These are the two essentials in the visual arts and crafts: first an awareness and observation of visible qualities and factors, and then a comparable awareness, and control, of the range of media in which an artist or craftsman can work. In the selection of some aspect of the visual world, of an appropriate medium, and in the attempt to interpret the one through the other, is the true self-discipline of free-expression, and the constraint of which Gide wrote: 'Art is always subject to some kind of constraint. To believe that the freer it is, the higher it rises, is the same as believing that what keeps the kite from rising is the string. . . . Art is born of constraint, lives on struggle, dies of freedom.'

In fact our proper acceptance of the challenge of a limitation liberates us, and it seems that frustration of some kind is necessary for the production of any considerable work of art or, for that matter, of any imaginative achievement by a child. From the evidence of their lives every creative artist has been subject to constraint – never the negative and destructive one of having to accept and reproduce an alien idiom, but one resulting either from material poverty, the physical conditions of his environment, the opinions and conventions of his society which may reject or even persecute him, or from the problems of his own personality and his never-ending struggle significantly to express his interests in terms of his medium. With the present patronage of the arts and the general tolerance of society which makes the material existence of an artist easier, the last, personal, constraint is often the only one which remains to animate creative work today. It is also the one most suspect both by the romantics who like to believe that a work of art is the result of some magical and inexplicable inspiration, as well as by the efficient rationalists who live by imposing their will upon others and upon their environment and who cannot credit that a sensitive approach to these and to media is either necessary or a true discipline. But because this constraint is fundamental in the work of any imaginative artist, it is, and always has been, not only inescapable and valid, but possibly the most potent of all. It is also fruitful in education where the constraints of neglect and rejection are out of the question.

There are few teachers today who do not encourage a child and give him care and consideration, but without effort, and even some frustration, a child feels that his education is too easy. Many a parent has heard the complaint of the 5-year-old after his first day at school: 'But I did nothing but play!', and the imaginative teaching of art and craft, with its demands upon his observation, his selection and control of media, is welcomed by a child as an antidote to the often over-indulgent concern for his comfort and well-being.

Through the effort of observation and the discipline of expressing this in terms of his medium, an artist or craftsman develops a deepening visual awareness and greater powers of creative imagination, which increase his perception and ability in other directions, including that of academic study. Intent observation is the basis of almost all accomplishment, and anyone well-practised in the visual arts truly sees – with interest, discernment and delight. He also handles tools and media purposefully and with sensibility, he gives his attention wholeheartedly to his work and, while he knows the satisfaction of attainment after difficulties, he is possessed of the restless enquiry which is forever urging him on to greater efforts. His powers of observation, initiative and controlled experiment are continually developing, and in consequence his resources, and indeed his whole personality, are enriched. If he observes, he wonders and questions, and being alive to his visual environment, he is apt to carry his interest into other fields of current topics and controversy, so that, whether we like it or not, in any community the artist and art student are likely to be among the most independent in their actions and beliefs.

A child is not a member of a different species, but another human being in the process of growing up, and I believe that when the disciplines and accomplishments of the visual arts are imaginatively presented to him, they are an essential part of his general education.

I will describe in turn each of these two basic efforts and their importance in education, but to avoid repetition I refer any reader who is interested in practical detail and application to my book 'Principles of Art Teaching'.

1. OBSERVATION

Observation is a requisite of all learning, and because it stimulates thought and understanding, it widens the scope and intensifies the quality of knowledge in every subject. Both the biologist and the novelist, for example, must observe nature and humanity, and the more sensitive their perception, the greater and more original their achievement.

Observation is no aimless relaxation, it is an active, outward-going effort of attention and a recognition of essential characteristics, which consequently enriches our subjective appreciation. We cannot assimilate every possible aspect of an object when we look at it, and because observation involves the selection of certain parts of what we see, and the relating of these according to our sensibility and purpose into a new form, it demands an imaginative relationship between us and the observed object, and it is in itself an imaginative act.

In his book *The Creative Imagination* Kenneth Barnes writes: 'To observe – to take notice of – is in some measure to experience, and observation therefore implies imagination. No knowledge is possible without an act of synthesis on the part of the knower, some kind of putting together, the imagining of a relationship. There can be no such thing as "mere" observation, a passive mind receiving an imprint. We bring something of ourselves to the discrimination of the most trivial object in the outside world.'

Observation is, however, interpreted in different ways, and for our generation whose perception has been dulled by an excess of images and by the fleeting, and usually wholly factual, cinema and television picture, true and attentive observation is difficult, and we substitute for it sentimental, associative or factual recognition.

When sight is sentimental, objective attention is replaced by subjective reactions and imagination degenerates into whimsy. Instead of accepting the impact of a visual experience and without prejudice acknowledging its especial characteristics, the observer recalls personal memories related to it, which arouse in him emotions of joy, sorrow, affection or disgust. Because it is un-familiar and therefore has no emotional associations, an original image is rejected as being horrible or out-rageous, and every chosen object or picture is standard-ised and reassuring. Art teaching is often sentimental, especially in the primary schools, and then a child learns to label some colours 'pretty', others 'ugly', to say 'lovely' to a picture of a silver birch tree but 'ugh' to one of a toad. He is taught to make a judgment based upon an emotional reaction and never to look with unprejudiced enjoyment, curiosity or respect.

As we grow older associative vision – the quick identi-fication and association of an object with our conditioned response to it – becomes a habit and sometimes a neces-sity. A housewife rarely pauses to look at the delicate structure of a cobweb, or a gardener at the form and colour of a thistle; to both they are undesirable, a threat to the plan of their domain and they must immediately be destroyed. More urgently, a child is frightened by a wasp or a snake, and he pays no attention to its shape, pattern and colour before he runs away or kills it.

Associative vision is implicit in our response to fashion of every kind. In that of clothes, we are persuaded by advertising to admire styles which later we consider ludicrous, while in the arts and in art education, the teacher, student and older child will accept only certain images and techniques, rejecting others because they do not derive from some current visual, sociological or psychological fashion. Yet the fashion which they in their turn establish may well seem absurd to succeeding generations. In the 1940s the disciples of picture-making condemned the carefully observed plant drawings of former decades; picture-making was later decried by teachers whose exclusive interest was in the analysis of natural form and that is now disdained by the hard-edge painters and the followers of pop, destructive and kinetic art, which will undoubtedly soon be superceded by some other idiom.

We have to take account of fashion, we enjoy it, and because it is the expression of the popular sentiment and understanding of our time we are inevitably influenced by it. But when we are dominated by it our vision is associative and limited; we have little imaginative comprehension and in education we forget that there is likely to be good in every method, so that the wisdom and achievement of former, and sometimes great, teachers is often carelessly ignored.

Factual recognition is another aspect of associative vision; it is the utilitarian and rational way of using our sense of sight which is undoubtedly necessary to each of us throughout our lives. When, for example, we are catching a bus, we have first to see that it is a bus and not a lorry which is approaching. Then we must make sure that it is the number we want and that it is safe to step out into the road. In this way we achieve our practical purpose and at every stage we can factually be proved right or wrong. But we have not seen the bus in terms of its bulk, colour, the pattern of its windows and doors and its spatial relationship with surrounding objects. The individual who does see these qualities and adds them to his visual vocabulary will have no immediate or measurable advantage; he may in fact miss the bus or lose his place in the queue. But he has made an effort of observation which nourishes his creative imagination, and which, with its inherent discipline and stimulus to his visual comprehension, has permanent value and far-reaching consequences out of all proportion to its simple origin.

In teaching it is difficult to discern any constructive purpose in sentimental vision and I believe that it should be discouraged, and while associative and factual recognition are practical necessities they should be known for what they are and never in education given undue importance or substituted for observation. All too often the progress, and even the intelligence, of a young child is measured by the speed with which he can identify and name objects, and charts and books are produced to hasten this ability still further. He is encouraged to take a quick superficial glance at everything around him, to label it or to relate it to some other experience, but rarely to look at it for its own sake and to enjoy its particular characteristics. If he does this he is slow to produce the conventional and impersonal comment, and so he is classified as backward. He is given little time to ponder and wonder at aspects of the visual world which are not directly related to identification, and his increasing skill at recognition outstrips, and finally submerges, his delight in objective looking. We should realise that, as William Walsh writes in *The Use of Imagination*: 'An image is more than a representation of an object: in it lurk dim meanings and indistinct connections which together form mental patterns long before the child can elaborate them rationally.' It is in these that his imaginative faculties are founded and from them that they develop.

For a young child, any over-encouragement of his rational progress is especially tragic because true observation, and consequently imaginative comprehension, are natural to him, and he knows little of the pressures of time and practical purpose. Intuitively he knows the disposition of adults and of his companions, and he responds spontaneously to their love, dislike, approval or disapproval. He identifies himself with the natural world; a stick is a playmate with a definite personality, an animal a friend to confide in, and he looks with absorbed attention at everything that comes his way – the slow, slimy progress of a snail, the pocked surface of an old wall, the turning of wheels and pistons in an engine, or the rivulets of water in a gutter with their miniature falls and eddies. He neither sentimentalises nor rationalises, for all is one with him and his experience, and when he draws or paints he often becomes the object, moving or making the appropriate noise – chuffing, for example, when he draws a train.

For his creative work, and again with spontaneous perception, he selects from what he has seen and felt qualities which confidently he reassembles and expresses in symbols. These are not independent of his environment – the outcome of some kind of infant mysticism – but they are his way of formalising his visual and emotional experience, so that the more he looks and has time to absorb what he sees, the richer and more personal will be his symbolism and the greater his ability and confidence in recording his ideas.

Many a 5-year-old child will draw a man with a round head, a triangular or rectangular body, with straight lines for arms and legs and dots for eyes, nose and mouth. Unless he is exceptionally perceptive he will persist in drawing this image until it becomes a stereotype, and he needs help, not with instructions how to draw, but with suggestions such as: 'Have you thought about ears? Have you noticed the shapes of eyes? Do you want to draw fingers?' If he ignores these remarks he is not ready to elaborate on his primary symbols, but as soon as he is capable of further observation his work will develop greater meaning both for himself and an observer.

For an infant, as well as for an older child, a subject which is apparently based upon memory or imagination nevertheless depends upon observation. When, for example, a child at school paints a picture of his mother, he is recording his recollected observation of her; in the same way his painting of a street derives from the houses, people and objects which he has seen on previous occasions, while his drawing of, for example, the Garden of Eden is all the more expressive if he has formerly observed tree and plant forms which he can recreate for this particular purpose. All his pictures are insignificant if he has no store of visual images with which to compose them, or if he relies upon memories of popular illustrations, and at school he should be provided with a wealth of visual material as well as the encouragement to observe and to consider subjects which have not so far occurred to him. A child has curiosity and humour, and far from preferring to be left to reproduce the conventional spacecraft or house-and-trees, he enjoys looking at an unusual object and considering an unexpected subject.

As well as the average view, with which he is familiar, both in his own picture-making and in book illustration, looking and working on a much smaller and a much larger scale stimulates his observation. A child loves to look closely at the intricacy of patterns in a kaleidoscope, and at the details of insects, grasses and lichens under a magnifying glass, while he welcomes a request to paint one object which will fill a whole sheet of paper – a huge sunflower for example – in which he will have space for all the details he can recollect.

As he grows mentally and physically, an infant's world of wonder gives way to an active, self-centred life. He loses his former security of unity with his surroundings, and he realises himself as an independent entity. His reactions and responses are determined by his wish to order and to dominate. A boy's dog, for example, previously his companion in its own right, is now the object of his sentimental affection – his dear little puppy – or it may have to justify its existence by playing some part in a game. He has little time for serene observation; he must be active, he must do and discover things on his own terms and within his especial interests, and he is quickly tired of any subject which is unrelated to these.

This activity and assertion can be exploited constructively in a child's imaginative education. He delights in the practice of the visual arts because it involves doing, and he responds eagerly to the responsibility of personal observation and expression. To him the whole visual world is exciting and waiting to be discovered, and with a careful, often cunning, choice of subject we can engage his interest and hold his attention, directing it to something which he might otherwise disregard, the patterns made by pylons, for instance, the colours in rusty metal, or the forms in machinery as well as the inexhaustible supply of those in natural objects. I have found that beach pebbles, flints and fossils, skeleton leaves, feathers and shells, whenever possible collected by the children themselves, are a sure stimulus to observation, especially for those who formerly have been visually disinterested.

On asking children for the 'things I remember' quoted in chapter 6, several gave me a conventional answer, based upon associative vision, which they thought would be acceptable or pretty. One nine-year-old girl said: 'the colour of blue-bell woods' but when I asked her if she had ever been to a blue-bell wood she said 'no', and after talking around the subject of memory she produced 'the colour of my bedroom curtains when the sun shines through them'. Especially today with so many standardised images around him, a child needs help in sincere and attentive observation, and a wisely chosen subject can break down the limitations of sentimental and associative vision.

Some theories on the education of young children which ignore the nature and importance of observation, have had a disastrous effect upon art teaching, divorcing it from imagination and transforming it into a purposeless pastime. In the past it was possible to neglect observation and yet to teach art to some effect. Although he may have been materially deprived, each child had more time and freedom from other distractions in which he could concentrate his attention upon personalities, objects and events, so that when he was told to paint what he wished, or when a subject, 'your holiday' or 'a fruit shop' for instance, was badly presented to him. he had visual resources from which he could create an expressive picture. But today he is bereft of both time and quiet, he is surrounded by standardised images and provided with occupations, his mind is cluttered with a miscellany of both important and trivial facts, and every art teacher should be fully aware of the necessity of focusing and extending every child's powers of observation, remembering that when we teach with due regard for these we are developing the imagination, but when, whatever our declared aim, we neglect them, we are destroying it. Pestalozzi believed that 'the fundamental axiom of the educative process is a continual reaction of the individual on his surroundings – a making of "the outer inner, and the inner outer".'

In adolescence a child's response is still self-centred, sentimental and emotional, but this is slowly replaced by a realisation of qualities independent of and exterior to, himself. He takes his first steps on the long road back to both an objective awareness and to an intuitive relationship with his environment. These were his unconscious attributes in infancy and they must become his conscious ones if he is as an adult to possess mature appreciation and imagination. He begins to enjoy listening to music and looking at pictures with an unprejudiced interest, and he discovers that in personal relationships he must adjust himself to the natures of others. He may react strongly for or against other people and events, but this is in proportion to, and proof of, his growing awareness. He is so much more sensitive to qualities in his environment and in the achievement of others that he is self-conscious about his own proficiency in the arts. He can see the discrepancy between his work and that which he admires, he may seek security in copying, and the teacher is plagued by the cry: 'I'm no good at art.'

But examples of art and craft, as well as the prose and poems, produced by many an older child prove that his considerable powers of observation can, with imaginative teaching, result in creative imagination, and that in his general education these are an invaluable means of expression and development. The belief, at one time generally accepted, that for all but the gifted child the ability to express ideas imaginatively disappears at puberty, was the result both of traditional art teaching with its insistence upon an exact technique and a representational result, as well as of the cult of child art which flourished in the 1920s and '30s and in which primitive symbolism was idealised. In both cases the ability and needs of most adolescents were disregarded. There are but few children of this age who are capable of skilful studies in perspective and of convential illustration, which were formerly demanded in the orthodox art class, while the child who has outgrown the naïve idiom of his infancy has no encouragement or help from a teacher whose appreciation is limited to that form of expression.

An imaginative teacher will meet these problems in the light of his particular sensibility and that of his time. Marion Richardson dealt with it no less successfully through plant drawing, the collection of natural objects and the matching of coloured wools than the teacher today who interests his class in shape, tone and colour divorced from representation.

In the art education of the secondary school child every effort has to be made to preserve and develop his powers of observation as well as his confidence in his creative work, assuring him that he is capable of producing something satisfying and worthwhile in one of the many aspects of the visual arts. We must cherish and foster his increasing awareness, so that instead of making him awkwardly self-conscious, it is the basis of his intent observation which will stimulate his creative imagination.

This is often difficult; the social and commercial pressures which I have described destroy a child's confidence at an ever-earlier age, making observation an incomprehensible, often an impossible, effort, so that he cannot concentrate his visual attention upon something which seems materially purposeless and unrewarding. Consequently the subject – by which I mean an observed object or situation, or an examination of abstract forms – in an art class is of even greater importance, for it can be used to give a child a deeper appreciation, a wider range of ability, and the confidence to explore a new realm of experience.

In his choice of a subject a teacher should always be concerned with extending individual perception and appreciation, and in his presentation of it he should as far as possible cater for every child's particular interest and sensibility. He can suggest a formal as well as a representational approach, and emphasise qualities of colour, surface and shape which each child can recreate in his own way. This choice and presentation must continually be reassessed, for although many a subject and approach which I have suggested for a younger child is as constructive for an older one, others are useless. A self-portrait, for example, happily undertaken by a young child is an embarrassment later in his school career, and if in the upper classes of a secondary school he is limited to pictorial subjects, he may lose all his interest. Yet his powers of observation can as well be educated through design or one of the crafts, for which he must perceive pattern and form in a variety of objects and then use these factors for his particular purpose. A teacher must never have a preconceived idea as to what is an appropriate subject or method, he has constantly to adapt these to the needs and development of every child, and whatever they may be they are justified if they help a child to look and to enjoy looking.

The results which emerge from the presentation of any subject should be various and surprising, notable for their diversity rather than their conformity. Observation is intensely personal, and although the preliminary effort can be stimulated and directed, each child must be free to select what are for him the significant qualities and to discover his own way of expressing them. No one, however great his own experience, can predict, or should presume to determine, how another individual will see and subsequently record what he has seen, and we must always encourage the effort of personal observation which is potent in the development of imagination.

To increase his ability to express his interests, emotions and ideas, every child, at every age, needs an expanding visual vocabulary which he can only acquire through personal observation. The art room, and ideally the school itself (which too often is characterless in the attempt to make it hygenic or tasteful) should be a glory of things which are fascinating to look at and to handle – natural, man-made and manufactured, ordinary and exotic, large and small, seen in section, in reflection, through a magnifying glass and a microscope, in natural and artificial light. The teacher should collect, and encourage his classes to collect, such objects and display them to their best advantage, and through his enthusiasm he will create a visual environment which will inspire in each child a love of looking and of handling for no purpose save that of wonder and delight.

THE EDUCATION OF IMAGINATION

The visual aids used in all subjects should not be, as they frequently are, and in spite of their name, a mere accumulation of images or formalised statements which appeal only to our rational intelligence, but a sensitive selection of evidence designed to stimulate visual interest and to heighten imaginative understanding through the sense of sight. I share with many others the dislike of standing to read close-packed print which would be better contained within a pamphlet or a book, and I am still further confused by obscure symbols and rows of geometrically-contrived figures or objects with perhaps the final one cut in half. But I do understand and remember more when I see a chart of good typographical design and when the aesthetic quality of an aptly chosen photograph or drawing substantiates the information it conveys.

In every school there should be, and in fact there often is, a collection of original works of art and craft, and each child should look at these quietly, intently, and with a wholly visual interest. We should not talk too much and encumber him with our own prejudices, or encourage him in the questions: 'What is it about?' and 'What does it mean?', but help him to use his eyes without sentimental or academic associations and to enjoy the shapes, colours, surfaces, the relations of these and how they have been used, either as an end in themselves or for a particular purpose.

If we are not to produce successive generations of dull-eyed adults we must educate each child to observe with imaginative comprehension and understanding, and for this he must have time, quiet and the possibility of being alone – all difficult to provide in schools with a crowded curriculum and anything up to 2,000 pupils. But time must be provided, generous and uncalculated, with no suggestion that there is anything more important to do. Quiet must be welcomed, not merely as an

121

absence of noise held for a few moments as one might hold one's breath, but as a positive and necessary condition which is enjoyable and in which the imaginative faculties can be rediscovered and develop. And to these should be added solitude, so that every child is sometimes alone, looking, assimilating visual qualities and adding them to his imaginative resources and vocabulary.

2. MEDIA

In the visual arts the choice and use of a medium are as necessary as observation to creative imagination, for these are the means of making a statement and of translating the original stimulus into a coherent and expressive two- or three-dimensional form. Ultimately the imaginative quality of the work depends upon the handling of the medium; it is the proof of visual effort, the evidence of sensibility, and another experience and discipline (often indeed a frustration) without which a work of art is impossible.

A medium can be used for either a utilitarian or an imaginative purpose, and handled so that it has either of these characteristics. As in the case of observation it is the utilitarian function – when it is used according to a formula and to achieve a predetermined result – which is the most readily appreciated today. It may be that cement is being applied to a wall, a plastic finish to a floor, paint to a how-to-do-it picture, or plaster is being poured into a pixie-making mould, but however skilful the user, the medium remains impersonal and anonymous. This is the legitimate and desired aim in building and decorating, but in the arts it is a denial of creative imagination.

When a medium is handled imaginatively, that is, with sensitive attention to its characteristics and a grateful acceptance of any unexpected attribute which may result from our use of it, it becomes a living substance, charged with latent possibilities and expressive both of its own nature and of the purpose of the artist. It is in itself a source of inspiration, and its physical substance is as much a stimulus to imaginative effort and development as the original object, emotion or idea: a shape, line, tone or an area of colour can, for example, take the place of an observed or recollected object as the start of a work of creative imagination, and in recent years the medium has to a great extent supplanted the image. From the first imprint on the paper or canvas, and the first shape in clay, wood, stone or any other three-dimensional material, the quality of the medium must be cherished and respected, for as soon as it is forced to conform to some preconceived technique it is lifeless, losing its power to animate the work as a whole.

Every work of art comes to life through the medium, and none can be termed imaginative unless the medium is an inextricable part of the creative process. However deeply felt the original stimulus may have been, it is the quality of the medium which determines its significance, and not the factual exactness, the extravagance or eccentricity with which the images are depicted or the work composed. The medium communicates through its colour, tone, line, form and texture which in themselves provide imaginative experience, while in their embodiment of the subject they convey imaginative truth. The organisation of these qualities are as absorbing in an Italian Renaissance painting as in a contemporary abstract or tachist one, while the handling of the paint in, for example, Rembrandt's portrait of an old woman, conveys not only the impact of a great work of art, but also an imaginative statement of old age in the depth of its emotion and condition. An exact representation of the same subject would give us no more than a factual description of a woman in a certain time and place.

The actual substance of his paint, a broken line, or an intensity of tone or colour may be unintentional, but it nevertheless results from the painter's sensibility. If he is working imaginatively, he welcomes such unforeseen qualities in his medium and allows them to alter or modify the form of his original intention. He requires all his previous experience to recognise and exploit them, and he also needs courage and initiative to work with new and often surprising elements. He is venturing into the uncertainty of the unknown and beyond that to the coherence of a work of creative imagination. This coherence is apparently simple and inevitable to an observer, but for an adult and an older child it is in fact the result of concentrated attention, struggle and sensitive selection.

Because a line, a colour, and a surface of tone or texture are in themselves imaginative and consequently creative, the drawings which are used in the currently fashionable creativity tests do no more than assess a child's ingenuity or memory of a popular illustration. It is impossible to declare that a line, shape, tone or colour is more or less creative and to give it a mark out of ten, and imagination is more often revealed in these qualities than in the actual drawing of a comic face or a whimsical animal. A sensitively drawn or painted tree, for example, may be more imaginative in its conception and interpretation in terms of the medium than a detailed picture of a dragon, but in any case our comprehension of creative imagination, whatever its form, depends upon the maturity of our personal appreciation which is also hard to assess. Creativity is far beyond the bounds of finite testing, for it is imaginative with infinite manifestations and forms of expression, and in some children it may only be revealed in the human terms of independent appreciation, values and sympathetic relationships.

However, just as language, spoken or written, is a manifestation and proof of significant thought, so the formalising of an idea by a child in terms of his medium provides a teacher with evidence of the existence and growth of his sensibility and creative imagination. Because of this, and not because it is what we personally like or expect him to produce, we can legitimately say that a child's work is 'good'. It supplies the proof of the development of his observation and of his ability to interpret this through his medium, and his 'good' work is as surprising and as much a visual revelation as that of any adult artist or craftsman.

A young child, and a well-taught older one, has the intuitive power to bring media to life. Confidently, un-selfconsciously, and with an innate respect for its qualities, he chooses and handles his medium to record his sensory and observed experience, and because he is able spontaneously to create a unity between his medium and his expression of the subject, his completed work communicates directly with an observer.

An infant may need help with the preliminary control of his medium, with, for example, the mixing of his paint so that it does not run into unmanageable puddles. He must be given this responsibility for if, because it is more convenient for the teacher, he is provided with ready-mixed paint, half the experience is denied him and he cannot be said to be painting in the full sense of the word. But with such responsibility he will with true creative absorption happily mix paint for the joy of handling it, and he may for some time have little interest in using it for making a picture. He is fascinated by the possible changes in colour, tone and thickness, and to him these are full of meaning; they may be important because they are his personal discovery, or they may suggest an object and be the beginning of his formal symbolism. He welcomes and accepts accidental developments in his media and allows them to determine the final form of his work. He is mastering the essentials of his art or craft and he is learning and progressing constructively through his own initiative, while through his experience, and in his own time he evolves a sure and personal idiom as recognisably his own as that of an adult.

Yet his environment and education, with their stress upon conformity and factual accuracy, are likely to destroy his spontaneous and imaginative response to media and his ability to use them expressively. For any child this is a deprivation, but drawing and painting are for an infant important alternatives to the spoken or written word as a means of communication and expression, while for an older, unintellectual child they are often the essential substitutes. We cannot healthily grow up in isolation one from another, and confidence, self-respect and consequently the whole course of development depend upon our ability to express and to communicate our feelings and ideas. Many a young child and one who is academically backward can do this through the visual arts, and if his interest and ability to work in different media are destroyed, he is denied his one opportunity for fruitful experience and accomplishment.

The roots of a child's development are in his confidence and some measure of success, which then encourage him in further effort. With imaginative teaching art and craft are activities in which any child may excel and acquire self-assurance. In an art class I am never able to distinguish the intellectual from the non-intellectual child (or often for that matter the conformist from the delinquent) so that each has the occasion to establish himself and to prove his worth without reference to his record in other subjects. This can be a decisive factor in the education of an otherwise unsuccessful child.

The expressive use of media usually remains with a child throughout his junior school years, but it disappears at an increasingly younger age and nowadays in the primary as well as in the secondary school a child may need help in overcoming the restrictions of a rigidly conventional approach. With a diffident infant (and sadly enough a five- or six-year-old can be anxiously conscious of a parent's command not to get dirty or to paint a pretty picture) this can be done by helping him to discover the exciting possibilities of mixing colour, how, for example, green can be made with black and yellow as well as blue and yellow, how adding white changes either of these still more, or how by scribbling with a soft chalk in different directions and with different pressures tones can describe various surfaces.

For both an infant and a junior school child the subject can give him a new interest in a medium. The drawing or painting of a slippery fish suggests a different use from that of a hedgehog or an owl, and I often ask a child to paint his whole picture in a limited range of colour, perhaps using only reds for a subject such as tropical birds, butterflies or flowers. An older junior can make patterns and pictures with cotton, string and wire, realising that a line need not only be drawn with a pencil and that fascinating lines can be made with any linear material. He can make his own tools for drawing and painting, with the feathery end of a feather as well as the quill, with cut and uncut straws and stems, and he can discover that he can print, not only with the usual lino or potato, but also with corks, nails, netting, leaves – in fact any thing with a suitable surface. Such experiments give him an interest in the quality of every medium, and the more he is absorbed in the possible

127

EDUCATION AND THE IMAGINATION

uses of each one, the more likely he is to develop a
personal and lively means of expressing his ideas.

The older the child, the more difficult it is to give
such help, and at a college of education many a student
is convinced that because he has not drawn, painted or
practised a craft since the age of 11 or 12, or because
he was 'no good at art' at school, he is incapable of
producing anything worthwhile, while at the other
extreme the facile student is unable to break away from
an impersonal commercialised cliche, recorded lifelessly
in paint or some other medium. But as soon as the one
has overcome his diffidence and the other his con-
servatism by discovering that he can sensitively exploit
his medium in his own way and for his own purpose, he
realises that he is capable of achieving a personal form
of imaginative expression, and that the enjoyment of
a work of art is a direct sensory experience related to
his senses of sight and touch, comparable to the appreciation of good cooking through the sense of taste, or of
music through that of hearing. For the diffident this is
surprising as well as satisfying, because he has formerly
believed that the visual arts involve esoteric practices
far beyond his understanding.

To give a student or child such confidence I believe
that, in common with all imaginative teaching, a simple
and unpretentious approach is the most constructive.
First I must have sympathy for the student's difficulties,
I must provide for his sensibility, and I must relate his
experiments with a certain medium to a subject which
will inspire various uses of it and which will reveal the
divergent qualities in, for instance, water and powder
colour, wood and clay. This subject, and my presentation of it, must not be intended to produce a particular
result which I consider acceptable, but must be within
the student's present comprehension, however limited
that may be, so that it is the basis of his further visual

128

comprehension and imagination, and not a useless imposition of a sophisticated technique and idiom upon his confusion of misapprehension and doubt. He needs to be provided with an observed subject or a carefully considered visual experiment, for left to himself without such a challenge he is either aimless, or fettered by his conventional style, but if I have asked him, for example, to base his exploration of the possibilities of ink and line upon a contorted root, or a clutter of scrap metal, or of gouache upon the colours in a flower or a stone, he has security in purposeful observation, while there are objective qualities to which I can refer in any comment or advice and which enable me to reply intelligibly to the retort: 'You say you like my work. I don't.'

An understanding of the nature of different media and tools and an ability to control and exploit them, is fundamental to work in any idiom and to a student's knowledge of teaching art to children. A subject or experiment provides the framework and first impetus, after which, with a sure confidence, a student or child can work out his interests in whatever way he pleases.

From his work in three-dimensional materials a child develops not only an appreciation of their characteristics and potential, but also spatial perception and understanding. This is an important and often neglected aspect of our sensory awareness. Many of us grow up with no realisation that objects exist in space and that a contained space is in itself a positive quality. A long, low room, for example, conveys a different sensation from a square or high one, and a circular hole from an elliptical. It seems that the more erudite we become, the more limited we are in our spatial comprehension. The art of unsophisticated peoples, the carvings of Africans or Eskimos, for instance, before they were influenced by western values, show considerable understanding of this kind, but in spite of our much-vaunted academic education we accept two-dimensional evidence as an adequate, if not the ultimate, description of our three-dimensional world. We recognise features on a surface turned towards us but we have no curiosity about what exists on the other side, or how one object is spatially related to another. We plan for the scientific exploration of space, but the greater our technical achievement, the less we seem to comprehend the reality of this aspect of the physical world, and while we live in space the sensory experience of it passes us by, so that imaginatively we are the poorer for having but a partial awareness of the circumstances of our existence.

I was first fully conscious of this lack of spatial perception when some years ago I asked teachers on a course to model in clay. Thoughtlessly I gave them little introduction, and every one of them proceeded to flatten the clay and then to scratch upon the thin, flapping surface lines which were intended to represent one side of the object they planned to model. Today I find that children are less spontaneous in their appreciation and handling of clay than they were twenty years ago and that they too are apt to start their so-called modelling by reducing the already three-dimensional lump to a flat one. This is likely to be the result of the innumerable two-dimensional images, in television, films and magazines, with which they are surrounded.

I am increasingly convinced that the handling and control of a variety of media and tools are among the most important means of releasing a student or child from his habitual prejudices and of substituting personal discovery and enjoyment which will lead to creative imagination. When, for instance, he finds that there are an infinite number of ways in which paint can be mixed, applied, related and contrasted, he becomes impatient of the conventional one which has formerly limited his development and awareness. At the same time he learns to respect and value his tools and media, and with growing confidence in his own ability and perception as well as with a fresh interest in the achievement of others, he acquires an aesthetic sensibility. Just as he enjoys watching a game, he may enjoy looking at a certain painting, sculpture or an example of craft, but it is only when he has played the game or handled the medium of the art or craft, realising both the problems and the possibilities, that his appreciation is at all profound. Such is his education and environment that while apparently looking he may not see anything of visual significance.

Proof of this can also be found in some of the art collections of the fortunate few who have inherited great paintings but whose choice of contemporary work is banal, or in the rebuilding of northern towns, whose dignified domestic architecture and individual planning can have made no impression upon the men and women who grew up in them and who now as local councillors are responsible for new plans which reveal a distressing ignorance of the important urban characteristics of well-related scale and space.

New materials, and a combination of them, revitalise a hackneyed subject or an overworked craft, re-establishing them in the main stream of a vigorous tradition, and today the crafts of weaving, embroidery and jewellery have been transformed in this way. A child's work will be enlivened and his sensibility increased by his personal discovery of natural and man-made materials and, as I have already suggested, as well as using the conventional media of the art class, he should be encouraged to find for himself any substance which he can use significantly. But we should remember that the greatest stimulus to his imaginative faculties is in the depth of his understanding of a medium and in his acceptance of its particular attributes, and that, rather than casually experimenting with a great number, it is better for a child to discover and enjoy the full possibilities of one or two with the appropriate tools, for as Whitehead stated: 'The best education is to be found in gaining the utmost information from the simplest apparatus.' For this a child must again have time and quiet, and his concentrated effort will give him that essential discipline which is most constructive when it is contained within his own experience and least when it is imposed from without.

Whatever the wish of a parent or teacher, it is impossible to force a child to be unhurried, quiet and alone, but when he is absorbed in drawing, painting or craftwork he is in a state of constructive solitude which is the antidote to loneliness, and he not only welcomes tranquillity as helpful to his occupation, but he begins to demand it as a necessary part of his everyday life. At the same time he is acquiring and realising the nature of discipline through his own interests.

This is the self-discipline which liberates him and gives him the opportunity for limitless imaginative development. It is gladly undertaken because it is an enthralling experience: he will discover and exploit unexpected qualities in his medium and consequently in his subject, eventually arriving at that simplicity and directness of individual expression which gives unity to any work of art.

I believe that these two disciplines of selective observation and of the purposeful handling of a medium are a potent means of educating the imaginative faculties of every child. They remain constant and they are always the basis of imaginative teaching, although because education reflects the values and achievements of the society of which it is a part, the idiom in which art is taught will change with social and aesthetic developments. Sixty years ago the sensitive teacher of plant drawings was as much concerned with them as Marian Richardson was later when she encouraged her classes in picture-making, or the teacher nowadays when he uses the methods of the basic art course.

When a child has the benefit of art teaching which gives rightful importance to both disciplines, he has advantages beyond a good aesthetic education, for he has experiences which offset those in contemporary life which discourage and destroy imagination. Today an urban child will to a great extent be insulated from the elements and from natural growth and materials; he will be burdened with an excess of utilitarian information; he will be hurried, crowded, and persuaded passively to conform to conventional, and often shoddy, standards. His work in the visual arts and crafts can restore his personal knowledge and understanding, for through it he learns to see and to regain an absorbed interest in his visual surroundings; he develops a respect and care for objects and materials, and an appreciation of quiet and solitude; he feels the need for sensory awareness and for doing things for himself and in his own way, and he begins to recognise quality and to be impatient of all that is false and inferior.

In his academic education there may be undue emphasis upon fragmentary facts, criticism, analysis and examinable results, while all the praise may be given to the quick-witted. In art and craft he learns to give his undivided objective attention, to put imaginative understanding before criticism, to respond to the whole of an experience, to record or express it in an integrated form and in some degree to comprehend the reality of imaginative truth.

8

Conclusion

A developed human being . . . is not merely a more highly individual-
ised individual. He has crossed the threshold of self-consciousness to a
new mode of thought, and as a result has achieved some degree of
conscious integration – integration of the self with the outer world of
men and nature, integration of the separate elements of the self with
each other.

> Sir Julian Huxley in his introduction to Pierre Teilhard
> de Chardin: *The Phenomenon of Man.*

I BELIEVE that this quotation describes an imaginative being and emphasises the inestimable importance
of educating the imagination.

When we are imaginative we wonder and perceive.
We are capable of ordered and concentrated attention;
before we analyse we construct, and we possess that
imaginative understanding with which the unintellectual man has powers of logical thought and without
which the supposedly clever one is stupid. We realise
our unique individuality and potential which we are
able to assert and establish even amongst the pressures
of automation and collectivisation. By our predomin-
antly rational values we have helped to determine the
characteristics of our society, and with greater imagination we could regenerate the unfortunate aspects of it,
for with this faculty every new achievement in science
and technology can be made to work for our best
interests, while without it any can be used to exploit
and degrade us.

Imagination animates all learning and it is present
in all accomplishment, providing that essential unity of
experience, understanding and expression which en-

CONCLUSION

ables us not only to comprehend the validity and permanence of imaginative truth, but also to achieve that two-fold integration of the self which de Chardin believes to be necessary to the evolution of civilised man.

If we are to further this ideal we, as teachers, must give our attention to the development of our own imaginative powers as well as to the proper and imaginative education of every child. With respect and understanding for his personality and needs, and for the fundamentals of our subject, we must pass on, not our prejudices, but the best of our experience and knowledge, encouraging each child in objective efforts of attention and awareness which will reflect back to enrich his imaginative being, so that with true confidence and by living outwardly he matures inwardly.

Through the perceptive teaching of all subjects the imaginative faculties can be rediscovered and educated, but I believe that with the arts we are most directly and potently successful. I have witnessed this in the visual arts, which, through observation and the purposeful handling of media, develop the relevant aspects of sensory awareness. If it were possible to ensure that in every school and throughout the curriculum each of the arts is practised with regard to its essential efforts, every child would have the opportunity of developing into a balanced and mature personality. The mathematician, for instance, need not be blind to the wonders of the visual world, the scientist to the literary, or the classicist to the musical, for the senses as well as the intellect of each would be educated, giving him greater understanding and sensibility, and, while he would be confident of his own developing powers, he would appreciate the achievement of others. He would be capable of independent thought and responsible judgment, creative not only in his chosen subject but also in his personal relationships and in his comprehension of, and contribution to, his environment, so that he becomes an increasingly enriched and mature individual. And at last there would be acknowledgement for the unacademic child, whose accomplishment would be applauded so that he would realise the worth of his effort and his dignity and place in the community.

I hope that in this book I have convincingly established that imagination can and should be educated, and that the experience which it gives us is more important and valid than any which we acquire through rational thought alone, so that a reader will recognise the truth of William Blake's statement: 'Imagination, the real and eternal World of which this Vegetable Universe is but a faint shadow.'